HOW TO FIND AN EXPERT

how to find an expert

Tips and tactics for finding an expert, from an accountant to a writer.

marc bockman

THE SUMMIT GROUP • FORT WORTH, TEXAS

THE SUMMIT GROUP
1227 West Magnolia, Suite 500
Fort Worth, Texas 76104

The guidelines in this book are well researched, but they *are* just guidelines. Use them along with, rather than instead of, your own good judgment. When you look for your own experts, you may sometimes find that certain people talk a better game than they play. Therefore, neither the author, the publisher, the researchers, nor those who graciously provided their own expertise for this book can be responsible if you choose the wrong person. But with this book in hand, the odds of finding the expert you need at the lowest possible cost and the least amount of trouble go up dramatically!

Printed in the United States of America.

94 95 96 97 98   5 4 3 2 1

Library of Congress Cataloging in Publication Data
Bockmon, Marc, 1943-
    How to find an expert / by Marc Bockmon.
        p.cm.
    ISBN 1-56530-160-9: $12.95
        1. Service industries—Handbooks, manuals, etc. 2. Professions—Handbooks, manuals, etc. 3. Specialists—Handbooks, manuals, etc. I. Title.
    HD9980.65.B63 1994
    338.4—dc20   94-24944
                                                             CIP

Book design by David Sims

"Everyone is ignorant—just on different subjects."

WILL ROGERS

*"**expert:** having, involving, or displaying special skill or knowledge derived from training or experience."*

Merriam Webster's Collegiate Dictionary
Tenth Edition

To the young lady who is now known as
Rebecca Michelle Morin,
but who always was and always will be
Daddy's little girl.

BIAS DISCLAIMER

I am in favor of ending all vestiges of sexism in the workplace. I endorse equal opportunity, equal pay, and equal respect. As an author, however, I find removing all so-called *sexist* language from our writing to be sort of like making an apple box out of a desk—you can do it, but it isn't very efficient or effective, and it makes for poor apple boxes and books. Some authors resort to using word-count to make certain they have used *she* as often as they've used *he,* and *woman* as oft as *man,* using chair*woman* in one instance and chair*man* in the other. Others replace gender-specific terms with gender-neutered terms, such as repair*person* and chair*person*. Lately, there has been a trend to remove mention of the person entirely, as in, "J. D. Jones, *chair* of XYZ Corporation, said yesterday that the sun would rise in the east." A *chair* said that? What is to become of us when desks, credenzas, and coffee tables begin making pronouncements?

Probably the least intrusive of the politically correct ways to handle the problem is to keep repeating *he or she* half the time and *she or he* the other half. For variety, one could also alternate between *he/she* and *she/he*. However, now that you know that my heart is right, I hope that even the most militant among you will forgive me if I use *he* instead of *he/she/she/he*, if for no other reason than the latter sounds more like laughter than communication. Rest assured, however, that whenever I talk about finding an expert, I am talking about finding an expert of *both sexes.*

MARC BOCKMON
Georgetown, Texas

Table of Contents

Acknowledgments

From the time I was twelve, all I ever wanted to do was write. My parents, naturally, did all they could to discourage me, for writing is a precarious profession at best. My father felt, as coach Bobby Knight would later quip, "We all learn to write in the second grade, but most of us go on to better things."

Later, when I began earning a comfortable living writing sales, safety, and training programs for a wide variety of businesses and organizations, my father seemed uncomfortable that all his dire predictions had failed to come to pass. Upon hearing a litany of my clients, he asked incredulously, "How can you write about all those things when you don't have a background in *any* of them?" I replied, "There is an *expert* in every company that really understands what they do for a living. Once I find my expert, I get him to explain it to *me*. Then all I have to do is explain it to others!"

That's what I've done in this book—found experts in every business and asked them to explain it to me so I can explain it to you. My staff and I interviewed *at least three experts* in each of more than sixty different businesses, asking them what they would look for if they needed someone in their profession. Some of their answers might surprise you. Some surprised us. Then, after I had written each profession up with an overview, tips and tactics, and a summary and conclusion, we went back and asked *one additional person in each profession to evaluate what we had learned, giving them an opportunity to add to it, if they desired.*

All in all, we conducted more than three hundred interviews covering sixty-four different professions. I could not, and did not even attempt to, do it alone. I would like to give special thanks to those whose devotion to the project went above and beyond the call to duty:

John Morin, my able assistant, associate, and friend, who quarterbacked the research teams, encouraged and cajoled me, and kept my feet to the fire.

Craig Lacy, who not only line-edited and critiqued the rough drafts, but also conducted many of the interviews himself.

Randy Sims, who did many of the original and follow-up interviews.

Paige Shaw, who doggedly kept on keeping on with interviews in spite of schedule conflicts and the heat of a Texas summer.

Mary Homerding, who came into the game in the "bottom of the ninth" and completed the last dozen-and-a-half interviews in record time.

Len Oszustowicz, my publisher, who not only caught my vision for this book, but also was so excited he convinced me to do it in an unprecedented four months!

Mike Towle, managing editor, who enthusiastically helped with layout, design, and suggestions.

Next, I would like to thank those who took time from their professions to tell us how *they* would go about finding an expert in their own fields. Their frank, honest answers to our questions, combined with my own experience gained by working with hundreds of corporations and organizations over the years, turned into overviews, tips and tactics, and summaries and conclusions. Sorting it all out wasn't always easy, because, sometimes, even the experts disagreed. For instance, one physician said, "I would *never* go to a doctor who took appointments!" Another physician, equally respected, said, "I would *never* go to a doctor who *didn't* take appointments!" One massage therapist felt that certain therapies were of little value; another felt those were of primary importance. Therefore, I had to judiciously choose from the information given and filter everything through our own experience and supplemental research. Consequently, while I believe all of those interviewed would agree that the information contained in the "Overview," "Tips and Tactics," and "Summary and Conclusion" for their profession is beneficial, I doubt if any single individual would agree with *every* single suggestion. However, aggregately, they have provided a unique inside view of what to look for when you need an expert in their professions. In fact, they have given us so much information that I not only feel confident that *I* could find an expert in any of these fields by following the guidelines, but that you could, too!

Having said all this, it gives me great pleasure to introduce, on the folowing pages, the experts who provided grist for our mills:

Accountant
Darren Bloch, CPA
Larry Fuller, CPA
Perry McDonald, CPA
Cindy Sims, CPA
Loreine Speakman, CPA

Air Conditioning and Heating Repair Service
Perry Joe Adams
Dave Chase
Ted Gilles
Ron Hughes
Tyler Milroy
Mac McMinn
Russell Trimble

Animal-Care Facility Operator
Kay Deans
Dr. R. L. Pruitt, D.V.M.
Dr. Paul Skellenger, D.V.M.

Appliance Repairman
Charles A. Howard
Jeannie Noble
Steve Schoby
Stephen Sparks
Bill Wilmes

Attorney
Robert Bruce
Jim Crumley
Lucy Hebron
Bruce Roberts

Automobile Repairman
Jim Harder
Timothy Elliott
Randy Rorter
Joseph J. Lescota

Banker
Bart Bade
Phil Martin
Daniel Preston
Sharron Sims
Gordon Tiner

Building Contractor
Steve Delt
Wayne Baranes
Robert Judd
Carl Morris
Ray Williams

Career Counselor
Mary Bass
Fred Fox
Loretta Gowen
Douglas Whatley

Carpet Cleaner
Gail Allen
Dudley Hill
Britt McCrummen
Mike Reed

Carpet Installer
Harold Plunk
John Surko
Charles Ripley
John Thompson

Caterer
Tom Armstrong
Carol Ekeredt
Carl Green
Becky Mosley

Child-Care Professional
Judy Carnahan
Suzanne Czap
LouAnn McMurray
Amber Purneda

Chiropractor
Catherine Antolak, D.C.
S. F. Cole, D.C.
Mike Maddox, D.C.

Computer Repairman
Bently Dedrick
Todd Hollaway
Charlie Sorrells
Robert Worrell

Dentist

Monty Buck, D.D.S.
Mack Hughes, D.D.S.
Mindy Matthes, D.D.S.
Richard Moore, D.D.S.
J. Robert Wells, D.D.S.

Detective

John Dunaway
Larry Elam
Kathy Griffin
Aimee Pickett

Doctor

John M. Clariday, M.D.
Allen H. Kline, M.D.
John Thomas, M.D., &
   Marilyn Thomas, R.N.
Yondell Moore, M.D.

Druggist

Fred Albert
Dale Brown
Gary Overbeck
Kelly Williams

Electrician

R. G. Good
Ronald Humphries
Eddie Ivy
Tom Walters

Electronic/TV Repairman

Bob Bond
Gigi Lee
Manny Silva
John Trovato

Estate Appraiser

Billie Godwin
Tom Keilman
Craig Lacy
Peggy Rowe
John Sauls

Family Counselor

Michael Bishop, Ph.D.,
   LPC, LMFT
Sally Cocker, LPC
Timothy J. Coody, LPC
Terry Selby, CSW

Fencing Contractor

Chris Britton
Richard Calhoun
Jimmy Gardner
Albie McLeroy

Financial Planner

Donald Ames
Chester Cowan
Bill Hudspeth
John Henry McDonald

Funeral Director

Roger Beaty
Paul Bohot
Brian Hillard
Bob Mooring

Gymnastics Instructor

Cindy Cardenas
Cindy Hawkins
Dianna Moore
Susan Smith

Hairstylist

Pam Bullard
Jennifer Frantangelo
Paula Martin
Nancy Roberts

Hearing Specialist

Jean Hutchins, Hearing
   Specialist
Billie Baker Swife, M.S., CCC-A
Kim Ringer, Audiologist
Angela Wooten, Audiologist

Home Builder (See Building
Contractors)

Hospital Staff

Barbara Beaird
Dell Conger
Harriet Downey
Dawn Gordon
Wendy Browder Kula
Vicki Morris

Income Tax Preparer

Becky Faust
Larry Fuller, CPA
Doug Scott

Insurance Agent
Vince Colvin
Ken Ewan
Craig Lacy
Jerry L. Sims
Owen Smith

Interior Designer/Decorator
Sherry Fielding
Ray Materavek
Judy Womack

Janitor/Maid
Wanda Dubbs
Haia Kheiry
Janice Johnson

Jeweler
Jesse Canon
Kim Kizer
Virginia Morales

Surveyor (Land)
Tommie Anderson
Steve Coalter
Scott Garanflow
Ken Gold
C. B. Thomson
Dana Markus-Wolf

Landscaper
Kerry Blackmon
Tom Kelm
Greg Mophet
Daniel Shopp

Lawn-Care Professional
Robb Gray
Steven Harp
Brock Lawson
Gary Ray

Locksmith
John Hernandez
Ron Parker
Wanda Robbins
Jack Miller

Mail Service
Pam Gorabia
Steve Koh
Carol Rachme
Marcia Stokes

Massage Therapist
John Mayberry
Marlene Merritt, R.M.T.
Mary Miles, R.M.T.
Greg Ray, R.M.T.

Maid (See "Janitor")

Nursing Home
Joyce Handorf
Carolyn LaPrade
Kay Reeves

Nutritionist
Cynthia Hanes, R.D., L.D.
James Heffley, Ph.D.,
  Biochemistry
Alexa Sparkman, R.D., L.D.
Michael Schiferl, A.D.A.

Optometrist
Dr. Laurie Sorrenson
Dr. T. D. McClenny

Painting Contractor
Virgil Conners
Allen F. Datson
Tim Hoskins
Ron Vernon

Photographer
Fred Conger
Mike Drago
Anne Harris
Tommy Holt
Bob Roberts
C. Smith

Plumber
Monte Anderson
Phil Francis
David Harrell
Jay Ingram
Billy Lewis

Printer
- Malcome Chilcote
- Steve Koh
- Michael Morgan
- Jeff Rabkin
- Bruce Test

Real Estate Agent
- Pat Crowley
- John Ferruzzo
- Sue Russell
- Diane Schrecengost

Remodeler
- Gilbert Bolding
- Wes Lokken
- T. A. Todd
- Ted Williams

Résumé Service
- Karen Kenter/Blumberg
- J. J. Marcff
- Jack Poston
- Raymond J. Terranella, Sr.

School (private)
- Light B. German, Ph.D.
- David Hoeft
- Amber Pruneda
- Michael Shephard, IECA
- Debbie Schuessler

Swimming Pool Contractor
- Ross Baarston
- Vince Colvin
- Larry Dehority
- Tom Johnson
- Ronnie Potts
- Scott Stolle

Tile Layer
- Manuel Castillo
- Paul Fair
- Jim Durham
- Kevin Lorino

Tanning Salon
- Chris Batten
- Daniel Gentry
- Joseph Levy
- Scott McGill
- Rebecca Morin
- Arlene Wesson

Travel Agency
- Pamela Chancy
- Ann Kirk
- Joe Lovoi
- Sally McCluskey

Veterinarian
- Clifford Bradshaw, D.V.M.
- Lewis Hanks, D.V.M.
- R. L. Pruitt, D.V.M.
- William B. Riddle, D.V.M.
- Paul Skellenger, D.V.M.

Wedding Consultant
- John & Juanita Benzer
- Michelle Chasnoff
- Roberta Speyer
- Janet Warren

Weight-Loss Consultant
- Sandy Adams
- Pam Choate
- Charlene Martin
- Bill Parsons

Writer
- Marc Bockmon
- H. Holland Harpool
- John M. Morin
- Ellis Posey

Special thanks to the thirty-four experts who also graciously shared their knowledge, yet chose to remain anonymous.

Introduction

Historians say Thomas Jefferson was the last "Renaissance man," the last who could know and understand the total of human knowledge. Since his day, knowledge has exploded, and the time is long past when any single individual could have a good, working knowledge of all professions. Therefore, even the most versatile among us needs experts. By experts, I don't mean that we need the foremost practitioners in the field, but experts that we can find easily, efficiently, cost-effectively, and *locally*. While we would agree that Dr. Michael DeBakey is an expert in medicine and Melvin Belli is an expert in law, the kind of expert we will show you how to find is the kind described in the tenth edition of *Merriam Webster's Collegiate Dictionary*:

> "expert 1. obs: EXPERIENCED 2: having, involving, or displaying special skill or knowledge derived from training or experience."

We all need experts because we live in an increasing complex society where margins for errors are decreasing while the cost of being wrong is increasing. Since we cannot do everything ourselves, we need to know who to turn to for answers. This book is designed to help you find an expert in the fields where you're most likely to need help.

To help you find the most qualified practitioner in your area, my staff and I asked our experts a very simple question:

"What would *you* look for if you needed someone in your profession?"

From their answers, we gleaned tips and tactics that we pass along to you. The sum total of their answers, plus our own observations and experiences, enabled me to write the overviews and conclusions.

This is a "general purpose" book, so our thrust is to help you find good, first-level experts. Still, we recognize that in today's complex world, some problems need to be "micromanaged" by specialists. If you follow these guidelines, you should be able to locate an expert who can handle most of your needs. If you have chosen wisely, *that* expert can, if need be, refer you to a specialist.

A good entry-level expert will never hesitate to refer you to another expert if the former can't help you. That's because *every expert has an expert.* This doesn't mean that the expert's expert is smarter—just that he or she has concentrated on a different area. For instance, when Dr. John Clariday, an expert family practitioner, saw that my wife, Marie, was not progressing as he had hoped, he referred her to an expert endocrinologist. When my optometrist, Dr. T. D. McClenny, saw a problem in one of my eyes that was outside his area of expertise, he referred me to a specialist who worked with people who had problems similar to mine.

It has been said that the three hardest words to say are, "I don't know." Experts never mind admitting that! In fact, once he suspects your problem is beyond his scope, he'll usually volunteer to send you to someone else, either in the same or in another firm. If he doesn't, and you suspect that your problem has exceeded the level of his expertise, he surely will do so at your request. That's why we don't cover specialties in this book. From a good M.D., you get a referral to a good surgeon. From a good optometrist, you get a referral to a good ophthalmologist. From a good dentist, you get a referral to a good orthodontist. From a good practicing attorney, you get a referral to a lawyer who is board certified in your area of need.

How do *you* find *your* expert?

My expert[1] advice is to read this book and begin looking for the experts you're most likely to need now! Then shelve the book where it's easy to find the next time you have an unexpected need for an expert. Better still, buy an extra copy and put it in your suitcase in case you need an expert when you're traveling.

....

[1] For the past nineteen years, I've earned a living as a "professional explainer," whose task it is to make complicated things sound simple and dull things sound exciting. In that capacity, I've written more than eight hundred programs for more than 180 different corporations and organizations, authored or coauthored a half-dozen books, and personally interviewed or reviewed the interviews of all the experts cited in this one!

Accountant

OVERVIEW

CPAs, like many other professionals, sell their time by the hour. You'll spend less for their time if you'll spend more of your own time in advance preparation. This rule not only applies when you *select* your accountant, but each time you send him your invoices, canceled checks, and other materials.

The first question most people ask is, "Do I need a large CPA firm or a small one?" It depends upon your needs. Larger firms tend to have the availability of a better breadth of experience and "upper-level" experts within the company. However, large firms can be more expensive and less personal. Smaller firms usually can take the time to get to know not only your business and investment strategies, but you, personally. If you have a small firm which doesn't mind either going outside for an expert or referring you to an expert whenever you have a question they can't answer, then you can often have the proverbial best of both worlds.

Whatever size firm you choose, you need to exercise care in selecting your personal accountant. It's a good sign if the accountant you are interviewing has other clients in your profession or similar professions, because then he will already be aware of the unique aspects of your business. Also, look for someone with certification in your area of need: CPA, tax professional, or enrolled agent. (An "enrolled agent" is licensed to practice before the IRS all the way to the Supreme Court.)

TIPS AND TACTICS

1. Ask friends and business associates.
As you ask, however, remember that we all have different needs. Give the most credence to the recommendations of those who have needs similar to your own.

2. Call several CPAs.
Tell them what you are looking for, and ask these questions:

- How long has your firm been in business? (Five years or more is preferred.)
- How long have *you* been in this business? (Five years or more is preferred.)
- How many CPE (continuing education) hours have you completed in the last year, and what did you study? (They are required to complete at least forty hours a year. If they completed more, or concentrated on your area of need, that is a good sign.)
- Can you give me some client references whose needs are similar to mine? (Be sure to check out the references!)
- Do you offer a free initial consultation so that we can get to know one another and discuss fees? (Most good ones will.)

■ If I'm audited, will you go with me and represent me?

3. Visit the most likely candidates.

A positive sign would be a willingness to take the time to fully discuss your needs, answer your questions, and look up any points of tax law for you. Negative signs would be evasiveness, being too busy to talk about your specific situation, and unwillingness to clarify an answer.

SUMMARY AND CONCLUSION

Benjamin Franklin once said, "In this world, nothing is certain but death and taxes." Not even the best accountants can help you avoid the inevitable, but they can keep you from paying a penny more in taxes than you owe, show you honest deductions, and plot you a path through a tax maze so complex that a former IRS head admitted to Congress that *even he didn't understand the tax laws*!

I figure that if the head of the IRS doesn't understand tax laws, what chance do I have? I also figure that when you're going through unfamiliar territory, it's good to have a guide that's been there before. If you feel that the accountant you are interviewing could be that person, hire him or her on the spot. On the other hand, if you feel uncomfortable in the interview process, then you're only going to be more uncomfortable when you have to start sharing personal and confidential information! The right person for you is one who is knowledgeable and personable.

Air Conditioning and Heating Repair Service

OVERVIEW

In the trade, it's known as the HVAC, or "Heating, Ventilating, and Air Conditioning," business. Next to medical services, we're probably more anxious about service to our comfort systems than anything else. To compound the problem, it seems as though the winds of fate conspire against us, and the AC only quits on the hottest day of the year and the heating on the coldest—which means that the HVAC people who had plenty of time to meet our needs in the spring and fall are now as busy as a one-armed paperhanger just when we need them most.

My grandmother used to say, "Beggars can't be choosers." If you don't choose an HVAC contractor before you need him, then you'll be placed in the *most uncomfortable* position of trying to interview prospects while the windows are melting from the summer sun or frost is forming on interior walls from the winter cold.

The best time to find *any* expert is on a *preneed* basis. If you begin looking for a HVAC dealer before you have a problem, you'll have no time constraints, and you'll find just the company to call when your HVAC system turns on you. (And it *will* turn on you, often when you least expcct it!)

TIPS AND TACTICS

1. Avoid service calls by planning ahead.

One of the leading causes of system failure is simply that the system is trying to pull air through a clogged filter! Remember the following: Repairs are expensive. Filters are cheap. So go change those filters right now and come back to the book when you're finished!

2. How do you find a good HVAC contractor?[2]

It's easier, of course, if you're calling from some place where the inside climate is under control. Ideally, this would be your own home, but if you've waited until you have an HVAC emergency, then it might be a good idea if you went somewhere where you're more comfortable to begin your search; otherwise, desperation might cause you to choose unwisely. In any event, here's what you do to find the right repairman:

....

[2] Did you really go and change your filters? I thought not! You also need to keep your coils clean and lubricated parts lubricated, if you want to save yourself trouble later. If you don't tend to these things regularly, you'll need to read on, because you're going to need an HVAC expert *sooner*, rather than *later*.

- *Check with your friends and neighbors.* Realize, of course, that if they were HVAC experts, they would be repairing their own systems. Since they're not experts, about all they can tell you is that someone nice came out, and the system worked when they left. They probably will not be able to tell you if the work done needed to be done and whether or not they were overcharged even if it did.[3]

- *Check the Yellow Pages.* If your state licenses HVAC contractors, look for ads with the license number. Look for the number of years the firm has been in business, and *particularly if your unit is under warranty*, look for a contractor authorized to carry your brand. A contractor that carries your brand can not only handle warranty, but will be very familiar with this unit and have an easy time obtaining needed parts. Also check the Yellow Pages to see which contractors belong to the ACCAI, an industry organization with high standards of service, training, and ethical conduct. Don't be misled by big, flashy Yellow Page or TV ads. These ads cost money, and that cost

....

[3] Back when I was slender and had hair, my wife called a repair person because the unit was making a "funny noise." A serviceman came out, solved the problem, and said, "The problem was your blower motor needed oiling! You need to call me every three months to oil it again." He adjusted the thermostat and, lo and behold, it quit working. When I got home, I went up, looked at the blower motor, and discovered it was a sealed unit and couldn't be oiled. When I called about the thermostat, I was told there'd be another service charge since that wasn't part of the original problem. I explained that I knew about the oil job, knew the thermostat had been sabotaged, and was going to call the BBB and the factory in an hour. The same repair person came out and, when confronted with his sabotage, merely smirked. He did, however, fix the thermostat problem he created. Naturally, I never called this particular company again. They subsequently went out of business.

must be passed along to customers. Many successful businesses rely on small ads and word of mouth.

Contact your utility company for recommendations. Compare their list to what you found out from your friends and the Yellow Page ads.

From the three lists you have (neighbors/Yellow Pages/utility), make a short list and contact the BBB to check for consumer complaints. Strike through anyone who hasn't solved their customer problems.

3. What to ask your HVAC contractor:

What do you charge for a service call?

What does the service call include?

Are you bonded and insured?

If I make an appointment, will you either keep that appointment or notify me at least an hour in advance that you're running late?

Do you guarantee your work? If so, how long is the guarantee?

Do you provide written estimates?

If the work you do doesn't solve the problem, am I obligated to pay for that work, or just the work that solves the problem?

4. What to do when they arrive:

Never allow any stranger into your home without proper identification. When your service technician arrives, he should introduce and identify himself. In addition, he should:

provide a quote before the work is done

provide a written estimate before he begins

■ point out the portion of the estimate that covers war-
ranties, damage waivers, etc., as well as advise you of
what is covered under your initial warranty

SUMMARY AND CONCLUSION

For a number of years, I wrote sales, training, and pro-
motional programs for a major manufacturer of HVAC
equipment. This particular manufacturer was very
proud of his equipment, training, and warranty programs, and set high standards for associated dealers. In
our long and mutually beneficial association, I had an
opportunity to interview hundreds and hundreds of
dealers. Like any other business, those that succeeded
over the long haul had certain things in common:

■ The HVAC contractor had high ethical standards.

■ The HVAC contractor exhibited a desire to serve, not
just a desire to *sell*.

■ The HVAC contractor made and kept appointments.

■ The contractor avoided tracking in dirt and debris and
carted off their own debris.

■ They handled callbacks quickly, efficiently, courteously, apologetically, and without charge.

However, in studying the industry for all those years, I've
learned that while all things a good dealer does have
value, not all have equal value. For instance, one dealer
always took time to wax the condensing unit cover. Customers were impressed, but a good shine added nothing
to the efficiency or life of the unit, and I'd hate to pay repair rates for cosmetic touches. I also consider service

and repair policies a waste of good money. While a service and repair policy *is* a form of insurance, it is an expensive form of insurance, generating more than 70 percent profit to the dealer.

The most important insurance comes free from the manufacturer when you purchase a new condensing (cooling) or furnace (heating) unit. The most vital and expensive parts of your HVAC system are the condenser on the air conditioner and the heat exchanger on the furnace. Depending upon which brand you choose, they usually carry a five- to ten-year manufacturer's warranty. That kind of warranty, coupled with a warranty you'll get on parts and labor when your HVAC contractor comes out to fix your immediate problem, should be a big enough umbrella.

Animal - Care Facility

OVERVIEW

If you're looking for medical care for your pet, turn to the veterinary section. Here, we'll deal with animal care as it relates to *grooming* and *boarding*. Incidentally, veterinarians are a good source of leads for grooming and boarding places and vice versa.[4]

Here's how to go about finding the right animal-care facility for your pet.

TIPS AND TACTICS

1. Get personal references.

Ask your vet. Ask your neighbor. Ask the humane society. If this doesn't get you a good reference, call some of the groomers listed in the Yellow Pages. If they sound nice, ask for references. (Remember, references must be checked, or they are of no value!)

....

[4] One time, we asked a vet to recommend a good animal-care facility, and we were quite pleased with his recommendation. However, on a lark, we asked the animal-care facility to recommend a good vet, and they recommended a different one! They didn't have anything bad to say about our vet, but it was obvious there was another they liked better! This obviously isn't a good example of "You scratch my back and I'll scratch yours." It is, however, a good example of integrity on both parts.

2. Look the place over.

Look for the same thing you would if it were a day-care center for your child. You want a place that's clean, where the personnel are courteous and helpful, and where the charges seem well cared for. The place should not smell of urine, nor should the pets seem frantic.

If you're boarding your pet, look at the area where it will be housed. You want a safe, clean place where your animal has room to exercise. When you enter the area where the pets are housed, any dogs will naturally start barking. Your first reaction will be, "My dog won't be able to get any rest if I place him here with all these noise-makers!" Relax. It's natural for dogs to bark when a strange person or a strange dog enters a room. They'll calm down later. (Incidentally, one of our sources tells us that some places sedate the dogs to keep them quiet, so *too quiet* a kennel might be a warning sign!)

Naturally, you want to make certain that the boarding place is *safe*. One winter's day, when it was below twenty degrees and a twelve- to fifteen-mile-an-hour wind was blowing, I drove by one kennel and found dogs out in a chain-link enclosure with no shelter and nothing to lie on but the cold concrete floor! Another time, a vet boarded my pet milk goat—and a pair of large dogs jumped a four-foot chain-link fence and killed her!

3. Make the first trip with your pet a short one.

If you're going to leave the pet at a new groomer, arrange to drop the pet off at the last possible moment and pick it up ASAP. If you're going to leave your pet in a kennel, try to make the first stay just overnight, so it will know you're coming back the next time you leave it there.

4. Let your pet tell you about the experience.

Owners get to know their pets rather well, and most of us can tell the difference between a pet that was just lonesome for us and one that was mistreated. We brought one of our poodles home from a new groomer, and for two days he just sat in a corner and stared off into space. Yet, he had been to many groomers before and had come home happy. The next time we went to take him there, he began trembling and whining when we stopped in front of the building. We relented and took him elsewhere, and he came home with what passes for a canine grin.

5. Report obvious signs of abuse or neglect.

Your local SPCA, local animal authority, and area vets should be notified of all abuse or neglect.

SUMMARY AND CONCLUSION

Our pets enjoy going to a good groomer. They come back happy, proud, and a bit self-satisfied, knowing they look good. (Our male becomes especially amorous when the female has just come from the groomer.) However, I don't know of any pets that really enjoy being boarded, even in the best place. Suddenly deprived of human companionship and familiar surroundings, they are placed in confined quarters with a bunch of strange animals, probably wondering if you're ever going to come and take them home.

For that reason, whenever possible, we leave our pets at home, in familiar surroundings, and ask a friend or neighbor to come in, check on them, let them out for a call of nature or for a romp, and then put them back. They are *still* deprived of your company, but at least they are home and seem contented in the knowledge that you are coming back for them.

If you must board your pets, we suggest that you do a couple of "trial nights" so that they can learn that you are coming back soon to pick them up. Also, leave their favorite toy for them to play with and the kind of food they usually eat. This will give them a link with home and make the stay a bit less stressful. If you select the right place, you can leave home for a few days in confident knowledge that your pets will be safe, comfortable, and reasonably contented. When you come home, well, that's the wonderful thing about pets—the moment they see you, all is forgiven!

Appliance Repairman

OVERVIEW

National organizations and franchises these days advertise that they repair anything and everything. *Usually*, these companies create a network of independent companies that operate from one switchboard to provide competent, if pricey, service. For those who prefer a more personal service, there are many independent organizations offering good services at prices that don't reflect the cost of expensive television advertising.

Major appliances have been around a long, long time and most of the changes have been for convenience or cosmetics. We buy a new unit because we want a convenience item the old unit didn't have, such as automatic defrosting, ice and water through the door, etc. Or, we buy a new unit because we want cosmetic changes, such as replacing round-topped units with square-topped ones, or we got rid of the coppertone color when avocado came out, then the avocado unit gave way to harvest gold, harvest gold to aqua, and aqua to almond, etc.

Yet, behind the changes made for convenience or cosmetics, the basic operation of the appliances themselves hasn't changed all that much. Major appliances, such as refrigerators, are designed to run for many, many years. In a recent episode of "The Secret Lives of Machines," they showed the progress of refrigerators by picking old ones out of junkyards and examining their inner workings for the cameras. Ironically, *all of the refrigerators brought in from the scrap heap still worked!* Owners had junked them because the bodies had worn, the linings had rusted, or because they needed larger units or new units to maintain a modern look in their kitchens!

In spite of new electronic components, most of the "guts" of washers, toasters, stoves, ovens, refrigerators, freezers, vacuum cleaners, etc., have been around a long time, and most of the things that can go wrong, and what one should do about it, are well known to those who repair them for a living. Consequently, very few repairmen will be surprised or stumped by a problem they find in your home—or hear described over your telephone. Therefore, even if you have a *portable* appliance, it makes sense to let your fingers do the walking and check out the repairman and the repair costs before you proceed.

TIPS AND TACTICS

1. Check the warranty.

Maybe the fates will smile on you, and parts and labor (or at least parts) will be covered by the warranty. If so, you'll want to call a *factory authorized* repair center.

2. Check the ads.

Look for firms that have been in business awhile and that handle your brand. Make a list of the firms that look good to you.

3. Check with your friends.

Ask them if they have had any experience with the companies you're considering.

4. Check the Better Business Bureau.

See if they've had any complaints.

5. Call the most likely candidates.

Ask to speak to someone in service. (A receptionist won't be able to diagnose your problem!)

Describe the problem you're having with your appliance as clearly and concisely as possible, and ask:

Have you dealt with problems like this before?

Are you familiar with this model?

Are you certified by the manufacturer for this brand? (This is not particularly important if yours is a common appliance or out of warranty.)

Do you have most parts in stock? If not, how difficult are they to obtain?

What do you charge for a service call?

What does the service call include? (Some service calls just include the trip, others include one-half hour to one hour's service.)

What is your best estimate of the cost to repair this item, *including parts, labor, time, travel (if any), and tax*?

If you follow the course of action just described and

still have the problem, do I have to pay for the repairs that you just mentioned or just the cost of actually solving the problem?

■ What kind of warranty do I get on the repairs? (Ninety days is typical. Some provide more, some less. One serviceman once told me that I got a "country guarantee," which he described as, "which means it should last a good, long time.")

SUMMARY AND CONCLUSION

One of the biggest complaints we've heard deals not with the repairs, but the repairmen. Too often, they've shown up hours late *or not at all,* without even the courtesy of a telephone call to advise. In the 1950s and 1960s, when Dad worked and Mom stayed home and cared for the home and children, there was usually someone home during the day. If a repairman came a few hours late, or even the next day, you were inconvenienced, but there was no real financial loss. Today, when both spouses are likely to be working away from home and one must take off to wait and wait and wait for a no-show repairman, tempers tend to flare. It's a good idea to say, "Okay, then I'll expect your repairman here tomorrow at __ o'clock. Now, since I'm taking off from work for this, I do expect a repairman around that time or a telephone call well in advance. Can you promise me that?"

A frequent repair ruse, favored by the telephone company, is, "We'll be there *sometime* Friday." When you try to pin them down, they say, "All we can say is that we'll be there *sometime* Friday. Will someone be home?" Since they're much less concerned about my wasted time than they are about their own, I always respond, "Someone will be home *sometime* Friday, but not *all the time* Friday. Would you like to pick an exact time so your repairman won't make a trip for nothing?" Invariably, this gets me a two- or three-hour corridor. Frankly, since no one can tell how long it'll take to repair any given item, you can't expect much better.

When the repair person arrives, see to it that he writes on the ticket the *exact problem you described.* After the work is done, ask him to write down everything he did and every part replaced. This gives you recourse should the problem persist. Also, retain any repaired parts that aren't needed in exchange, *just in case* the replacement didn't solve the problem!

Considering the life expectancy of major appliances, I would be very uncomfortable if I got a strong sales pitch from the repairman to buy a new one, unless he doesn't sell new appliances.[5] If I felt the least bit uncomfortable, I'd take his estimate and call someone else to ask if it was reasonable and if, in fact, the appliance was worth repairing.

....

[5] We called Charles Howard, an appliance repairman in the area where we live, to look at a very ancient automatic washing machine that wasn't working properly and sounded like the B-26s did in Vietnam right before the wings fell off. He said, "I repaired the immediate problem, but your bearings are bad and your tub is rusting. These things can all be repaired, but I don't think it would be cost-efficient. I've got your immediate problem fixed, but if I were you, I'd watch the sale ads for washers." Since Mr. Howard was factory-trained, had seventeen years experience, and didn't sell new appliances, we took his advice to heart.

When a repairman says you'll save money replacing a *small* appliance (coffeepot, toaster, blender, mixer, etc.) rather than repairing it, he's probably right. The fact is, modern assembly lines are so fast and efficient that a new item can often be assembled for less money than an old one can be disassembled, repaired, and reassembled on the repair bench. This is especially true if the factory, as so many are today, is in a country where wages cost less than American manufacturers have to pay for social security, workman's comp, and unemployment insurance.

Attorney

OVERVIEW

There are more attorneys in New York City *alone* than there are in the entire United Kingdom, and law schools are churning out 20 percent more than are needed to replace those who retire. To find employment, some attorneys are aggressively advertising on daytime TV, partly because it's less expensive than prime time and partly because some figure if you're home during the day, maybe you were injured or fired and there might be a case in it.

The surplus of attorneys, aggressive attorney advertising, and today's litigious society has made members of this valued and important profession the butt of many jokes, and lawyers are often vilified, scorned, and slanged. Yet, because we live in a society both maintained and constrained by laws, we must have *lawyers* to make certain that we stay within the law whenever we can and to see that we are accorded all the safeguards of the law when we are accused of violating the law or making a mistake with civil consequences.

When looking for an attorney, keep in mind the old Persian proverb: "The buyer needs a thousand eyes, the seller none." Ignore hard-sell advertising and look for listings in the Yellow Pages or newspapers that are tasteful, modest in size, and professional looking. Good attorneys, like good doctors, get most of their business by referrals. Big, explosive, brassy ads seem to have a hint of desperation about them that is best ignored.

In spite of all the jokes and jibes tossed at attorneys, most of us require the services of a good attorney at some point in our lives, and many lawyers are genuinely nice, caring people. (No, I wouldn't have minded if my sister married one. In fact, a sister-in-law *is* an attorney!) The information below was gleaned from interviews with reputable attorneys we respect.

TIPS AND TACTICS

1. Find the attorney you need; don't let him find you!

While many good attorneys advertise, so do many mediocre ones, so ignore the clever copy and the promises that you'll get wealthy because you were fired or injured. If you need an attorney because of those reasons or because you've been indicted for a crime or need to draw up a will or agreement, don't be influenced by the firm with the biggest ad budget. Instead, call the local or state bar association and ask for a list of attorneys in your area.

Most attorneys, like most physicians, are "general practitioners." That is, they do all kinds of legal work from criminal cases to wills, probate, contracts, etc. In Texas and many other states, their ads will carry a slogan that says something like, "Not certified by the Board of Legal Specialization." That does not mean that they aren't highly qualified attorneys, but that they're "general practitioners" like your family doctor. Most of the time, you'll save money and get just as good representation from a general purpose attorney. However, if you have a specific need, then you might wish to choose an attorney who is specialized in, say, criminal law, tax law, personal injury, etc. If so, ask your bar association to send you a list of attorneys who specialize in that field. The bar association will send you a list of attorneys in good standing. Of course, the bar association does not always exclude attorneys who've been reprimanded by the bar. And just because the bar doesn't know anything *bad* about an attorney, it doesn't necessarily follow that they know anything *good,* either! If you have a legal problem that might wind up in court, get to know the court reporters and ask them who wins that kind of case. Don't choose an attorney solely on fees. After all, you save nothing if you lose the case!

2. Know the fees up front.

Attorneys sell their knowledge and their time. Before you do anything else, briefly outline your needs and discuss fees. When you discuss fees, remember the adage, "Unwritten agreements aren't worth the paper they're written on." Most attorneys are honest, but there can be honest disagreements over what was said. *Get your fees agreed upon, and get them in writing.*

Attorneys can bill you several ways:

A. *"The meter is running."* To make certain they get paid

for all the time invested in your project, most attorneys prefer to bill you for services as they are provided. Therefore, every time you call to ask a question, or the attorney calls someone to ask a question, or he looks up a point of law, interviews a witness, etc., the meter is turned on. In addition, most attorneys want to recoup their "hard costs" such as typing services, long distance calls, photocopies, faxes, etc. If you have a simple case, open billing means that you'll save money if the case goes smoothly. On the other hand, if the case is complex, you could have a very, very hefty legal bill as there is no cap on your charges. (Joke: Know the difference between an attorney and a boxing referee? The referee doesn't get paid more if the fight lasts longer!)

B. *Flat fees.* Some attorneys will promise you a flat fee. Usually, if you're getting something simple, such as a will drawn, a power of attorney, etc., the flat fee will hold. After all, they're merely plugging your name and numbers into a piece of computer software. In more complex cases, however, some attorneys come back later and say that they'll need more money to finish the work. The only way you can protect yourself in this case is to have a written agreement beforehand that clearly states that the flat fee covers *all contingencies* and *all services.* Incidentally, the "flat fee" should go into a trust fund instead of the lawyer's account. The money should be withdrawn only when the work is performed.

C. A piece of the action. Often, if you are suing someone for damages, an attorney will agree to work for a percentage of any anticipated settlement. Some attorneys take 33 percent, and some 40 percent. Naturally, you want one who takes the lesser amount. You also want it in writing that the percentage is *all the attorney* will be paid and that you won't be billed for *anything* else, whether you win or lose.

3. Ask about previous experience in similar cases.

If an attorney says, "Oh, yes, I've tried several such cases!" ask if he won or lost the case. (If it's a civil matter, in addition to asking if he won or lost, ask him which side *he* was on! If he won for the opposing side, you'll want to know what steps he will take to see that your side doesn't lose this time!)

4. Ask about others who will work on your case.

Many attorneys use legal assistants to reduce their own workload. There is nothing wrong with this practice, but you do have a right to meet the person who will be assisting your attorney and to expect her to be certified. The support staff should be courteous and competent. Make certain that the fees for any legal assistants are included in the *written* estimate you receive after the initial consultation. Naturally, the assistant's time should not be billed at the same rate as the attorney's.

5. Be prepared to answer questions.

A good attorney will ask you as many questions as you ask him to clarify just what you need and where you stand. An attorney who does not ask a lot of questions may be uncertain just which questions to ask, or, worse, he may be disinterested.

6. Use your head.

If the attorney seems evasive, press for details. If the law he quotes seems unreasonable, ask to see the statute. (If the attorney says, "I don't have time to look it up right now," call the local bar association, and ask the same question.)

SUMMARY AND CONCLUSION

Many civil cases that go to court could have been settled with far less trouble and money by arbitration or negotiation. I've seen people pay an attorney five thousand dollars when they could have solved the problem directly for five hundred. If you're suing or being sued, remember the words of Jesus, "Settle matters quickly with your adversary who is taking you to court. Do it while you are still with him on the way, or he may hand you over to the judge, and the judge may hand you over to the officer, and you may be thrown into prison." Know your rights, but make the courts a system of *last resort* instead of *first resort*. However, when you *must* resort to the law, choose your attorney as carefully as you would your family physician.

Automobile Repairman

OVERVIEW

Few among us understand our highly sophisticated, highly complicated automobiles. Today's cars go farther than ever on a gallon of gasoline, and in addition to providing safe, reliable, comfortable transportation, everything is automated, from the shifting of gears to opening and closing the trunk and gas lids, raising and lowering the windows and radio antenna, to climate control, ride height, and programming for the radio, CD, and tape players. Some cars are even equipped with wireless transmitters that will allow you to start the engine and position your seat as you start toward the car. Others come equipped with voice-activated cellular telephones and fax machines.

The automobile has always been a part of American life, but today it's not only a pleasure vehicle, it's a home and/or an office on wheels. Understandably, we feel threatened and a bit put upon when ours turns on us. Unfortunately, our lack of understanding about how cars work and our frustration that they have ceased to work sometimes make us distrustful of those we depend on to fix the problem and restore our transportation.

Relax. In spite of a few highly publicized stories, most mechanics are honest. However, some are better than others. Here's how you go about getting a good, honest mechanic who'll get you back on the road as quickly and economically as possible.

TIPS AND TACTICS

1. Get recommendations.

Ask your friends who they use and if the repairs were done right *the first time*. Ask if the estimate given at the time of diagnosis was reasonably close to their final bill. If you don't know anyone to ask, pick several repair shops at random from the Yellow Pages, and call the Better Business Bureau to see if they have any complaints against them.

2. Call the shops. Ask questions such as these:

- What is your labor rate?
- How long have you been in business? (Tenure *is* important.)
- Are your mechanics ASE (Automotive Service Excellence) qualified? (ASE certifies mechanics in *complete* automotive mechanical repair: engine, transmission, air conditioning, etc.)
- Do you charge for a diagnosis of my problem? If the problem is simple, many won't. If, however, it is

unusual or elusive and they must use sophisticated diagnostic equipment, most will charge you for the service. Today's sophisticated mechanic, like today's sophisticated surgeon, likes to run some tests before he starts opening up and replacing parts! It's always less expensive to pay for diagnostics than it is to pay for unnecessary repairs and wasted time.

3. Visit the repair places that get passing grades from your telephone review.

If it's a small shop, you'll probably be talking to the mechanic that will do the actual work. If it's a larger firm, you'll probably speak to the service technician who usually is either a mechanic or has undergone diagnostic training. (One manufacturer trains its service techs to write down *exactly what the customer says.* In other words, if you say, "My car goes *boing, boing, bonk*!" they write down, "Car goes boing, boing, bonk."). While you're there, do the following:

- Explain your problem. The mechanic, or service technician, should take notes, ask questions, and listen carefully to your answers.
- Ask for a written diagnosis and estimate. Then ask, "If the things you repair don't fix my car or solve the problem, will I have to pay for the unnecessary repair?" If you get a "yes" answer, take the diagnosis and estimate elsewhere. Ironically, while we have to pay physicians and surgeons even if they don't fix the problem, mechanics usually only charge for the things they do that actually solve the problem!

■ Ask them to save your old parts, so they can show you what went wrong. (Ask in a tone that indicates you are *interested*, not that you're distrusting!)

4. If you feel uncomfortable, or would like to comparison shop, take the diagnosis and estimate elsewhere.

Ask them the same questions, and keep visiting other facilities until you feel confident that you've found one who can do the work to your satisfaction.

5. Resist a "hard sell."

If a mechanic or service technician tries to "sell" you, scratches his head and rattles off a long list of things it "might" be, or uses any pressure or scare tactics—go elsewhere.

SUMMARY AND CONCLUSION

After all the questions above have been asked, the question in many minds is, "Do I go to a dealership or an independent garage?" It's a simple question, and unfortunately, like most simple questions, there is no simple answer. From our own investigations, *all other things being equal*, we'd give a slight edge to a dealership. All mechanics charge by the hour, and dealer's rates are usually a bit higher than independents. However, many dealers are required to operate from a "flat rate manual" on repairs. In other words, if the factory says it will take an hour to repair an item, then you're billed for an hour—*regardless of how long the mechanic takes.* Also, dealers usually have all the parts you'll need *in stock*, while most independents will have to stop work while someone goes to an auto parts store (or a dealer) and buys the part.

Another advantage dealers have is that their volume in both new and used cars means they'll have the latest electronic diagnostic equipment that can provide a printout of just what is wrong. *Some* independents have this equipment, too, but virtually all dealers do.

Strangely, some customers don't want to pay for electronic diagnosis. As one put it, "I don't want to pay them to find out what's wrong; I just want to pay them to fix it!" Well, that can get expensive. I know of one independent mechanic who kept replacing parts on a late-model car, and, yet, the problem persisted. Because he was buying his parts at a dealership, he finally told the dealer, "I've charged this customer seven hundred dollars for parts and labor, and I still haven't been able to find the problem. What would you charge me to do an electronic diagnosis?" The dealer said, "As good a parts customer as you are, I won't charge you anything." They put the car on the diagnostic machine and found that the problem was a seven-dollar part!

Ironically, *both the part and labor were under warranty!"* (Incidentally, the dealer was able to get the mechanic and his customer their money back on the unneeded parts!) Admittedly, this is an extreme case. Here are some "rule of thumb" guidelines on where to go for what!

■ **Go to an independent repair shop for basic, nonwarranty repairs.** This would include brake work, alignment, tune-up, etc. Exhaust problems can usually be repaired by an exhaust specialist for less than a dealer pays for the parts. Electrical problems can usually be solved by an electronics specialist in less time than a mechanic would require. A good tip is to let specialty shops perform only their specialty. For instance, take muffler work to a muffler shop, brake work to a brake shop, get tires and alignment at a tire store.

■ **Go to a dealer for all warranty work and major problems.** Electronic (as opposed to electrical) problems are often intermittent and can sometimes only be traced by a process of elimination. For instance, when using a diagnostic flowchart, a technician may encounter a reading that says, "Replace with (a) good known part." The "good known part" may cost five hundred dollars and not fix the problem. If so, the dealership can simply return the part to inventory and continue looking.

So, do you go to a dealership or an independent for an auto repair? It depends on the problem, and it depends on the mechanic you choose. If the problem is complex, make certain that you choose a place that has ASE-certified mechanics, the latest diagnostic tools, and people you trust.

Banker

OVERVIEW

There was a time when the family banker was as much a part of the community as the family doctor, butcher, or baker. He knew and was known by everyone in the town. Banking was a personal business. When you needed a loan, the banker not only looked at your balance sheet and credit report, he also looked at *you*, your roots, your record, and your reputation. A family banker always gave good financial advice and would stretch a point based on who you were.

Today's regulations limit some of the freedom bankers once had when it comes to lending. Also, many small, independent banks have been absorbed by megabanks with branches spread throughout the region, state, or even the nation, and some institutions seem to have lost the personal touch. Yet, whether you choose a smaller, independent bank or a branch of a large institution, it is *still possible to have a personal banker.*

The first thing you have to do is decide what kind of bank you want. Small, independent banks pride them-

selves on personal service. Conglomerate banks pride themselves on convenience, enabling you to make a deposit or withdrawal at any of several locations, even across the country!

And it is possible to find a personal banker at a big bank. I found one when we moved across the state and needed to borrow a substantial amount to purchase a home.

The following tips and tactics will help ferret out what kind of bank you're dealing with and help you locate a personal banker, whether you're using a branch bank or an independent.

TIPS AND TACTICS

1. Ask friends.

Ask several people you trust to recommend a bank *and a banker*. Then go and visit those banks, beginning with the *most recommended*. Whether or not you can get a recommendation, follow the steps below.

2. Make certain that deposits are federally insured.

It is a rare bank, indeed, that isn't insured by the FDIC, *but they do exist*. However, there are limits to what the FDIC will insure in a given account. Should your deposits exceed that amount, you might wish to open several accounts to guarantee the security of your funds.

3. Case the joint.

A bank is like any other business. They have something to sell. In order to compete successfully, they have to attract customers. What kind of job do they do when you go in? Are they warm and friendly or cold and sterile? Pick warm and friendly.

4. Don't go to the new accounts person.

Usually, the person in charge of new accounts is warm, friendly, and can efficiently fill out the forms to open your account. Usually, they are also inexperienced. Any banker will agree to hold your money and charge you for the privilege of writing checks on your account. You want one who will uphold your case should you have a banking need. To find that person, walk up to whoever is in charge of dispensing information and move directly to tip No. 5.

5. *Ask to speak to the (or a) loan officer.*

Once you're in his or her office, say, "I'm really not in the market for a loan right now, but I am in the market for a bank. I'd like you to tell me about your bank." Then ask the following questions:

- How long has the bank been here? You want a bank with tenure.
- How long have you been with the bank? You want a banker with tenure.
- What kind of loans do you like to make? [6]
- Do you finance automobiles, home improvements, home mortgages? Do you prefer to do business loans or personal loans? What percentage of each do you do?
- What percentage of the loans from your bank (or your branch) are made in the local community? (*If it's not at least 50 percent, then they are not building up the community of which they are a part.*) Scriptures say that our hearts are where our money is, so if their heart isn't in the community, look elsewhere. One of my

....

[6] Some banks would prefer to make an $800,000 loan to a business rather than one hundred $8,000 loans for cars or home improvements. Choose a bank that prefers to lend in the area where you're most likely to have a need.

small-town banks has a billboard that says, "Investing in Main Street, not Wall Street." That's the kind of attitude this customer likes! If you feel differently, then find a bank that thinks like you do!

6. *Ask how long it takes to approve a loan.*

Twenty-four hours is good; two to three days isn't.

7. *Ask about charges and rates.*

Particularly ask about charges on checking accounts. Ask about loan rates, too. Although these rates vary from time to time, once you know what they charge, you can comparison shop. Remember, however, that a bank is in business to make money. If they're significantly lower than the competition on one thing, they're likely to be significantly higher on others. As they say in carnivals, "If you can't make a profit on the peanuts, then you have to make it on the popcorn. If you can't make it on the popcorn, then you make it on the peanuts."

8. *Don't be totally swayed by costs.*

We all want to save money, but don't let minor differences in charges be the determining factor in choosing a bank. My own personal bankers will approve loans on the spot, over the telephone. They will transfer funds for me, work out details on loans for me, and are always friendly, and helpful. When I moved, they even went out of their way to find me a good bank and a great banker in my new location. I recommended this bank to a friend of mine who was moving to the area, but he chose another one instead. His reason? "I liked your bank and your banker, but they were a *quarter of a point* higher on my

$15,000 car loan! I got out my calculator and ran the numbers. *The difference was $1.78 per month!* My bank and my banker are worth a lot more than that to me!

9. Choose a banker you like.

People are all different, and bankers are just people. If the banker you're interviewing is cold, uncommunicative, in a hurry, or rude *when you don't need anything*, it doesn't take much imagination to figure how he will act *when you do need something*. Cold fish belong in a meat market, not in a bank. If you don't like the person, be warm and friendly and thank him for his time and try elsewhere.

10. Get a goof-proof account.

Your bank might charge you for an inadvertent overdraft, but you never, never, never want them to return a check marked ISF (insufficient funds). A really wonderful personal banker will do this for you as a matter of course. A good banker will do it if it's part of a premium package for an extra fee. Unless you're one of these very organized people (in other words, not a writer of books), you'll appreciate the fact that the bank is not only looking out for your money and best interests, but your credit and credibility as well!

SUMMARY AND CONCLUSION

Although banks today provide many financial services, the two primary ones are checking and lending. If you are choosing a bank only to have a checking account, then go for the one which pays the highest interest on

deposits and charges the lowest fees, but if you're looking for an institution to provide you with complete banking services and sound financial advice, take the time to
choose a *personal* banker before you open an account.
You don't want to be in the position of having a financial
need *and then* finding the bank is unwilling to work with
you! I have personal bankers at small, independent
banks and one in a large conglomerate. Good, personal
bankers like these are a rare species, but fortunately they
are not endangered. You can find yours if you try, and a
little time and trouble spent now will save you a lot of
time and trouble in the future.

Building Contractor

OVERVIEW

For generations, we've been told that "a home is your largest lifetime investment." Since my wife's last automobile cost almost as much as our first home, I'm not certain that's true anymore, as a lifetime of cars can easily outstrip the cost of a lifetime of a house. However, both the best and the worst car you'll ever own will eventually go to the junkyard to be reborn as a tuna can or a pipe wrench, while a properly constructed home *can* last a lifetime.

Unfortunately, in spite of building codes, some homes are not built as though they were expected to last even the life of the mortgage. I've seen broken boards wrapped with filament tape used for studs, cracked concrete, and irregular walls go up only to be hidden by wallboard, plaster, paint, and carpet. In addition to sloppy workmanship, the trend in home building has been toward increasingly cheaper materials and methods. Instead of nailing, some builders are using staples. Instead of plywood, some builders are using wafer board. When the house is finished out, you can't tell the difference, but the difference might become apparent over time. For instance, after recent hurricanes in Florida, inspectors found that houses built the traditional way, with nails and plywood, stood, while newer homes built using staples and wafer board were destroyed.

We once bought a new home that, unbeknownst to us, had aluminum wiring. The builder saved a few hundred dollars—solving the problem cost many multiples of that. The same builder used tar paper for a shower pan in our tile shower. He saved thirty dollars off the cost of a lead or plastic pan. When the shower began to leak, we had to pay twelve hundred dollars to have the tiles removed, a decent pan put in, and the tiles replaced. If I had been asked if I would pay extra to have copper wiring, a decent shower pan, a high-efficiency air conditioner, and decent building materials, I would have answered yes. I wasn't asked. The price was *a bit* lower than it might have been—yet I paid a hefty premium later!

When we moved, I made certain I had a good shower pan and copper wiring. But I didn't totally escape the penalty of builder shortcuts. In our back lawn was a quaint little footbridge over a small ditch that diverted water from all the rest of the homes in the area through my backyard into the lake down below. Naturally, I assumed the footbridge was made of treated lumber, because the difference in cost is slight, and working with treated lumber costs no more. It wasn't. In three years, the boards and even the posts had rotted and needed to be replaced. So I had the cost of the original materials and construction, plus the cost of new materials and construction. Would I have paid the difference if asked?

Certainly. But I wasn't asked. You see, both times, *I bought a house that was built—not a house that was built for me!*

How do you protect yourself if you're buying a ready-built home? You can poke around and ask questions, you can get a licensed inspector or structural engineer to check it, you can purchase a home warranty, or all of the above. Even then, there are no guarantees.

My poking around, after the house was built, revealed nothing but what the builder wanted revealed. An inspector *probably* would have caught the aluminum wiring, but would have had no way to check the tar paper underneath the shower tiles and no reason to check the redwood-stained footbridge. A warranty would have run out before the shower pan leaked, the aluminum wiring caused a fire, or the footbridge rotted.

The safest way to get exactly the quality you want is to have your home built for you. All you have to do is find a builder who is as concerned about his or her reputation as you about your home. "Ah, therein lies the rub!" Here are some tips and tactics to help you find such a building contractor!

TIPS AND TACTICS

1. Wander around.

Hewlett Packard, one of the most successful American-owned electronics companies, has a program called MBWA, "Management by Wandering Around." Visit houses under construction. Check the quality of the builder's work. Does he build with wafer board and staples or plywood and nails? Do you see obvious flaws that the builder figures will be covered by paint, plaster, paneling, or carpet later? Note the names of the builders whose work you admire and those you wouldn't hire to build your doghouse.

2. Check 'em out.

Call or visit several builders whose work you admire. Tell them that you want to build a home, vacation cottage, or whatever, and that you've seen some of their work and would like to find out more about the firm. Ask:

How long have you been in business? How long in this area?

Are you bonded? (This covers any damage he does to your property.)

Are you insured? (This covers any injuries he or his subs may have while on your property.)

May I have a copy of your financial statement? (This shows that he has the funds to do the job.)

May I have your banking references? (This shows he has the credit history to deserve your trust.)

May I have a list of people you've built homes (or whatever) for in my price range? (This shows he can perform in the area where you require him to.)

Many times, we are reluctant to ask such personal questions, but these are nothing like the personal questions the builder and mortgage company will be asking you! No reputable builder will be upset that you've asked for credentials. If he seems upset or defensive, that's your clue to look elsewhere. If you feel comfortable after the interview, you'll want to:

- Run a credit check on the builder.
- Check him out with the Better Business Bureau.
- Check him with both the NAHB (National Association of Home Builders) and your local home builders' association.
- Call others he's built for and ask them if the job was done on time, to their satisfaction, and if the final price came in reasonably close to the estimate. You'll also want to ask about any problems they might have had and whether or not they were amicably resolved.

SUMMARY AND CONCLUSION

There is probably no area of real estate more fraught with danger than interim financing of a home. One highly reputable contractor we interviewed said, "Fifty percent of building contractors have stiffed someone. If he doesn't pay subcontractors, *you* are responsible." He is right. If you pay the contractor, and he doesn't pay his subcontractors, *you are liable.* One hears horror stories in which the would-be homeowner has paid 100 percent of the contractor's bills and is still left with half a house and a bunch of angry subcontractors who are threatening to sue. Ironically, the way the law works most places, if you write the contractor a hot check, you have committed a criminal act. If the contractor takes your money and doesn't perform, you have a civil matter! (No, it isn't fair, but surely you learned life wasn't fair long before now!)

What is the best way to avoid a problem? First of all, resist high pressure and smooth talk—and investigate, investigate, investigate. Do the same kind of background investigation on your building contractor that a lender would do on you! Next, establish in advance at what stages different amounts will be paid. *Pay for nothing in advance; pay for each stage as it is completed.* Before you hand over any interim payment, get a signed, notarized statement from the building contractor that he has paid all his subcontractors and suppliers for all work done to that date.

He can still lie, but if he signs this and hasn't paid his subs and suppliers, he has committed *fraud* and now faces criminal as well as civil action! This can be a very big deterrent to ripping you off! One home builder we know had scammed several buyers and lenders, and delayed civil trials with apparent impunity until one sharp savings and loan officer required him to sign the sworn affidavit that all his suppliers had been paid to that point. When it turned out that the suppliers *had not been paid to that point,* that little piece of paper was sufficient to put the unscrupulous builder behind bars!

Do not make the final payment as soon as the last work is done. Have it understood up front that the final payment will not be made until *thirty days after the work is completed.* Although you have a signed, notarized affidavit that the subcontractors and suppliers have all been paid, this will give anyone missed time to contact you.

Best bet? Even if you have the cash to pay for the job, make arrangements with a lending institution to handle the disbursements for you. They will have set guidelines that show at what stage a certain percentage of the job will be done and are much more experienced in evaluating progress and in dealing with contractors. Understand, even with all the "safeguards" in place, you can still get stuck. A builder, for instance, could declare bankruptcy and leave you with a half-finished house. However, if you've only paid for the work done to date, you can find another builder to complete the project. Next time, of course, you'll be *even more* careful!

Career Counselor

OVERVIEW

A few years ago, I saw a book titled, *How to Find What You're Best At.* I thought at the time, Obviously, it's not grammar! I mean, for a sentence like that, there is no parole! However, the book had helpful hints to guide the reader in taking her areas of interest and translating them into potential professions. Without professional guidance, we can waste years in the wrong profession. I know. I've been there. I've done that. However, as difficult as it is to change careers in life's midstream (I was thirty-two), there is a worse-case scenario: We could spend our entire working life doing something we don't enjoy.

Joe DiMaggio was a failure as a fisherman, but he loved to play baseball and became one of the all-time greats. Dr. Conan Doyle was a failure as a physician, but he loved to write, and his Sherlock Holmes stories thrill us even today! The right career counselor can help you find "what you're best at"—even if it's not grammar.

A *career counselor* is not the same as an *employment counselor.* An employment counselor helps you *find a job.* A career counselor helps you find your area of interest and locate a career field that will relate to that interest. While some might help you find that job, most will merely tell you where those jobs can be found. Most provide testing, to gauge your interests and abilities, and counseling. Most work on a flat fee up front, though some will charge in steps, allowing you to quit when you feel you have all the data you need.

One counselor we interviewed said, "We get two kinds of people—those with no job, and people who are totally frustrated with their jobs." Whichever kind of person you are, here are some ways our experts say to locate the career counselor who can help you.

TIPS AND TACTICS

1. Look for experience.
Check the Yellow Pages and make some telephone calls. Ask:

- Does our state require licensing of career counselors? (Some do, others don't.)
- What are the *minimum* qualifications to be a career counselor in this state?
- How long has your firm been in business? (Five years or better is good.)
- How much experience do your counselors have?
- Do you belong to any professional associations of counselors? (For instance, many career counselors in Texas belong to the Texas Counseling Association.)

2. Ask for references.
A good career counselor should be willing to give you the names of former clients who have been through their procedure and were helped by the process. Ideally, of course, in addition to references for the firm,

you'll get some for your career counselor. Be sure to ask if the counselor *or the counseling firm* has any expertise in the career path you find most interesting.[7] Ask to meet the counselor before you sign to pay for any services. Your counselor should share his credentials and explain, in detail, how he will help you.

3. Sign nothing on the spot.

You'll naturally want time to look at their materials, think about your initial interview, check references, and call the Better Business Bureau before you decide.

4. Expect some testing.

One counselor said, "I have sixty-three hours of tests available covering everything from aptitude to achievement to work sample to vocational testing. Our purpose, however, is not to test people into oblivion and then give them the printed analysis based on their answers. Our purpose is to select the right tests to reveal to us and to the client areas of interest and expertise."

5. Expect good counseling.

You should be individually coached and guided so you know:

■ which career field most interests you

....

[7] Some career counselors do specialize, some dealing with engineers, others with accountants, etc. Loretta Gowen, one of the career counselors we interviewed, specializes in helping people with disabilities return to the workforce. She works with her clients to see where they are and need to be in five areas:

1. Personnel assessment: attitudes, self-management ability, motivation, and self-esteem.

2. Communication skills: telephone, written, person-to-person.

3. Group effectiveness: interpersonal skills, negotiating skills, team-building skills.

4. Leadership skills: goal setting, negotiation, problem solving, trustworthiness, respect for others.

5. Job search skills: career definition, résumé writing, job interviewing.

- how to design a career profile
- how to write a good résumé
- what you need to do next

6. *Warning signs:*

- counselors who promise to find you a higher paying job in a new career (Unless you're making very little now, it is highly unlikely that you can start out in a new career making more money.)
- counselors who won't talk about their own credentials
- counselors who are haughty, hurried, or talk in clichés

SUMMARY AND CONCLUSION

In the front matter of this book there is a quote from Will Rogers that bears repeating: "*Everyone is ignorant, just on different subjects.*" Whenever we hire an expert, we are admitting, "Hey, I'm ignorant on the subject on which you're an expert!" That's okay. If you want to learn, there are no dumb questions. The only thing dumb is *not asking questions.*

Many times, professionals, such as physicians, attorneys, and career counselors, who deal with our deep-seated hopes, dreams, and fears do not realize that they intimidate us. *They* do not want it that way, nor is it in our own best interest to allow it to happen. Should you sense your career counselor is talking down to you, courteously remind yourself (and him) that *you are the employer, and he is the employee. You are paying his salary.* Therefore, his task is to make you feel comfortable, to guide and direct. Your obligation is to honestly reveal what you want and need, and to question, probe, and make certain that you both understand what you're seeking.

I spent eleven very profitable years in a career I did not enjoy. And because I had carefully planned my transition to my new writing career, I made more money the first year as a writer than I had my last year as a salesman. I jumped careers and never looked back. You can too—if you're dedicated, if you're motivated, and if you get the right career advice!

Carpet Cleaner

OVERVIEW

Before you start looking for a carpet cleaner, look at your carpet. Carpets can be made of many fibers (wool, nylon, polyester, and acrylic are common ones), and each requires a different type of equipment. For instance, you cannot steam-clean wool carpet, and you cannot brush-clean acrylic. Beware of someone new in the business who has been sold (or is renting) a wonder machine that, he is convinced, can be all things to all carpets. Carpet is expensive, and so is carpet installation. If the wrong person tries to clean it the wrong way, you might end up with carpet that is discolored, has lost its luster, or, in some cases, has even shrunk!

TIPS AND TACTICS

1. Ask your neighbors!

Dirty carpet is unsightly, but not getting it cleaned isn't an immediate threat like not having plumbing or air conditioning or heating repaired. If you're new in the neighborhood, knock on some doors and say, "Hi, I'm _____ (fill in your name), your new neighbor. Do you know a good carpet cleaning service?" It's a great way to get acquainted, because people naturally open up when they're asked to share their opinion or expertise.

2. Check the Yellow Pages.

Look for firms that have a physical address and have been in business for several years.

3. Call the most likely prospects.

Tell them what the problem is, how many square feet of carpet you have, and *the fiber*. If the problem is a stain, try to identify the "it" for them. Ask if they're members of the IICUC (International Institute Carpet and Upholstery Certification).

4. Ask for an estimate.

Bid a fond adieu to someone who arrives at your door, and in spite of accurate information on your part, tries to charge you substantially more than the estimate.

5. Ask if they're bonded and if their work is guaranteed.

No one can guarantee to remove a stain, but they should be able to guarantee the overall quality of their work, and that neither furniture nor carpet will be damaged by their workers or processes.

6. Ask for references.

Remember, references that aren't checked might as well not exist.

7. Call the Better Business Bureau.

Ask if they have any complaints against the company.

SUMMARY AND CONCLUSION

Some of those we interviewed told us that most of those in the carpet *cleaning* business are former carpet *layers* who often begin with an ad, a truck, and a rented machine, and the only training they have is what they'll get from their first few customers.[8] If so, there is nothing wrong with that, as we Americans take pride in our ability to lift ourselves up by our bootstraps. However, you want to make certain that your carpet cleaner has taken time to learn the business and isn't planning to practice on your carpet. True, carpet cleaning isn't brain surgery, but before someone starts pouring and brushing chemicals in your $38-a-square-yard carpet, you want to make certain that your job doesn't make "one-in-a-row" for him.

Don't be sucked in by someone who calls you on the phone, rings your doorbell, or hangs a flyer on your doorknob with just a phone number to call. He *may well be gone by the time you discover that your carpet is ruined!* Of course, many reputable and established businesses do telemarketing and door-to-door solicitation, so the fact that someone calls or knocks on your door *alone* isn't a reason to avoid them. However, you should not commit until you've checked their credentials. You want a firm with a physical address, a proven track record, and a good reputation, and is bonded. (If the firm isn't well established, ask to *see* the bond!)

Beware of companies who apply heavy pressure to change the agreement once they've begun. Halfway

....

[8] However, one carpet cleaner, who did not wish to be quoted by name, took very strong exception to that statement and said that most didn't come from the carpet installation business but were Mom and Pop entrepreneurs who didn't need a shop as all cleaning is done on site. Reminds one of the American proverb, "A man with a watch always knows what time it is. A man with two watches is never certain." Or, perhaps, more accurately, the Jewish proverb my friend Jay Shear used to quote: "Wherever you have four Jews, you'll have five opinions!"

through a job, one company once told me, "We charge extra for moving furniture!" I merely raised an eyebrow and replied, "Oh? And when you gave me your price on the telephone, did you expect to find the furniture suspended from the ceiling?" He hesitated, laughed, and finished the job without any further reference to an increased price. He did a nice job. But the attempt to gouge me for extra money ended any chance he had for my repeat business or my recommendation.

Carpet Installer

OVERVIEW

Turn back and read the entire section on carpet cleaning. It will give you some insight into the carpet business.

A handful of mills make carpet. Most of them make several grades, and the better grades, installed correctly over the correct pads, will provide years of comfort and service. However, anyone can print up flyers, make phone calls, or even put up a sign saying, "Carpet Sales and Installation," and they're off and running. Some only have sample books and a few "end rolls" and "remnants" and place their order when you place yours. Some will misrepresent the quality of the carpet they're selling, and you can pay a premium price for what you think is a premium product only to find that you paid for a Cadillac Seville and bought a Honda Civic.

Of course, whatever price you pay for your carpet, you want it properly installed. Unfortunately, carpet installation isn't as easy as it looks. Doing the job right requires the right skills, the right training, the right tools, and the right techniques. Following are tips and tactics to help you find an installer you can trust for both carpet selection and installation.

TIPS AND TACTICS

1. Ask around.

The purchase of carpet isn't an emergency, so take the time to ask friends whose carpet you admire where they got theirs, if they are happy with it, and if they were pleased with the service they got from the dealer.

2. Check 'em out.

Check the Yellow Pages and the newspapers for ads from the companies your neighbors recommended. Call and ask what brands they carry and, most especially, how long they've been in business. Call the Better Business Bureau and the Homebuilders Association. (Just because the Homebuilders Association hasn't heard of your dealer, it's not necessarily a negative. Some dealers don't bid on new construction work because the margins are so small.)

3. Decide what you want.

You want to be open-minded when you visit the showroom, but you should determine your preliminary carpet criteria: color, durability, stain resistance needed, and wearability beforehand.

4. Measure the area to be carpeted.

The dealer you select will need to do this anyway, and you'll probably need more than your measurements will indicate, due to the fact that you won't want to do a room out of the scraps from previous rooms. Still, your measurement will give a preliminary idea of how many square yards you'll need so you can comparison shop.

5. Visit a showroom.

The showroom should be clean, neat, orderly, and professional looking. Explain to the dealer just what you have in mind. A good dealer will never pressure you to make a decision, but will ask questions to clarify in both your minds what you want, need, and can afford. (Dealers will come to you, but since anyone can obtain a sample book, it's a good idea to look at the dealer's physical location somewhere in the buying process.)

6. Answer and ask questions.

The dealer will probably ask you:

What is your color scheme?

What is your budget?

What style do you like?

How long do you want it to last? (Yes, this is a reasonable question. A person who is planning to move or remodel in three years usually isn't interested in paying a premium for long-wearing carpet, while a person who is settled would probably like to buy what he wants and not worry about replacement for a long time.)

You should ask the dealer:

Are you an *authorized* dealer? (Some manufacturers only warranty carpet purchased from an authorized dealer.)

Do *your* people do the installation, or do you rely on a subcontractor?

How much experience does the installer have? How much experience will *my crew* have?

Is the installer bonded and insured?

Does *your firm* stand behind the installation?

Who is taking *personal responsibility* for this job?

■ What recourse do I have if the job is done poorly?

- Can you give me some recent references involving the crew that would be installing my carpet?

7. Be easily turned off.

The more pressure I receive ("This is only on sale today!" "If you decide today, I can install it tomorrow, otherwise, you'll have to wait a month!"), the quicker I leave. Besides sales pressure, other turnoffs are:

- a dealer who doesn't ask questions
- a dealer who doesn't give specific answers (or a dealer whose answers leave you even more confused)
- a dealer who is unable to confirm a time to come out and measure your home or do your work
- a dealer who "talks down" to you
- a dealer who is evasive
- a dealer who doesn't return phone calls or keep appointments

8. Get it in writing.

If you and the dealer come to terms on everything else, make an appointment for them to come to your home and actually measure the area to be carpeted. They should be able to explain any discrepancy between your estimate of the number of square yards and theirs. (For instance, carpet comes on a twelve-foot roll. If you're carpeting an eleven-by-eleven-foot room, there's going to be some waste. There isn't a lot you can do with a one-foot strip eleven feet long!)

SUMMARY AND CONCLUSION

No matter how comfortable you feel, *check prices*. It

never hurts to get two bids and compare them, although if the difference in price is small, you're probably better off going with the dealer that you feel most comfortable with. After all, any business has to make a profit in order to survive, and the guy that has the lowest price might not be around later if you have a problem.

If, after all the preparation, you should have problems with the quality of product or installation, *begin by being nice*. My mom used to say, "You can catch more bees with honey than you can with vinegar." In the unlikely event being nice doesn't work, you can always try something else later.

Caterer

OVERVIEW

Whether it's a formal French dinner served in an elegant dining room with silver and china, and a fine Bordeaux served in crystal stemware; or a folksy backyard barbecue on picnic tables with paper plates, plastic utensils, and keg beer in Styrofoam cups, when we arrange for a catered affair, we expect good food, good service, and hassle-free dining.

Whatever your culinary tastes, here are some tips to get just what you want!

TIPS AND TACTICS

1. Ask around.
Ask neighbors, friends, and church and civic groups for the names of caterers they've used with good results.

2. Ask for references.
Remember, *obtaining references isn't enough. You have to check them.* Find out if the food and service were up to expectations, and if the estimated price was the final price.

3. Look for a menu match.
A good chef can prepare just about everything, but just as you wouldn't go into the most accommodating Italian restaurant and ask them to prepare sauerbraten,

neither should you expect a caterer to do something outside his realm of experience. If you want barbecue, look for a good barbecue restaurant that caters. If you want continental cuisine, then look for someone specializing in that.

4. Look for time in business.

Time was when experience could be determined by how long a place had been in business. However, while the *business* might have been around since 1895, the *current owners and management* might have only been around for a few weeks. So, when you pick a place that's been in business a long time, call and ask, "How long has the person in charge been there? How about the staff members?"

5. Ask about the chef.

Experienced management, servers, and food preparers are nice, but the key to the food is the chef. Ask how much experience the chef has. If you're looking for a gourmet meal, ask what schools he attended. (Even if you don't know one school from another, if the answer is "none," you'll learn something.)

6. Ask what they do best.

While a good caterer will be willing to work with you, you're always on solid ground if your needs match up with what he does best.

7. Ask who is responsible.

An answer you don't want is, "The chef is responsible for the menu, the driver for getting it there at the right temperature, the servers for setting up, the—" etc., etc. You want *one person* who will take total charge, *and you want that person at the party*!

8. Ask how long it takes to set up and tear down.

You'll have to arrange your gathering so that the caterers and guests don't clash before or after the meal.

9. If you want something different, arrange for it well in advance.

If you have a favorite recipe, most caterers will prepare it for you. Find out whether or not your caterer will work with you.

10. Get in writing just what services and products are included and the total cost involved.

Good relationships have been ruined by misunderstandings. "*Everyone* knows that gratuity and corkage aren't included in the price!" Avoid misunderstandings by having an estimate that says, "This price includes *everything.*"

SUMMARY AND CONCLUSION

Most caterers will quote you an inclusive price based *per person*. Naturally, if you're using your own plates, tableware, and glasses, and simply want the food delivered and the serving pieces picked up afterward, the cost will be much less than if you wish them to serve, and furnish tables, napkins, dishes, tableware, etc. Be certain that everything *they are to do* and everything *you are to pay* is down in writing! You do not want to have to debate billing while your party is in progress.

Child-Care Professional

OVERVIEW

The high cost of living (or, as some would say, the high cost of high living) has put many mothers who might have preferred to stay home with their children into the labor force. Current tax law enables us to deduct child care from our taxes *only* if the care isn't provided by a relative. The bottom line is that *even if you have a close relative who loves and wants to keep your child, you only get a tax break if your child is cared for by strangers—which means professional day care.*

The workers at the day-care center might, and probably do, like working with children. However, keep in mind that caring for your child is their *job* and that you are paying them to perform this task. They are employed by you and the other parents. Don't be one of those parents who is so grateful to find a nearby day-care center that has room for your child that you forget to do what any good employer would do: check references, check backgrounds, and interview those involved to see if they are qualified!

TIPS AND TACTICS

1. Find a day care with your values.

The day-care worker(s) will be spending forty or fifty hours a week with your young, impressionable child. Look for a day care that not only houses, entertains, and educates, but one that will build on foundations you feel are important.

2. Talk to friends with children in day care.

Ask what their impressions are. Is parental input encouraged and heeded? How do their children feel about the facility? Do they look forward to each new day, or do they leave in the morning as though they were going to the gallows? Do they come home happy, or tired, irritated, and grumpy?

3. Check out the choices.

In most states, licensed day-care centers must meet minimum standards for child development, education, fire safety, health, and sanitation. Contact your state licensing department and the Better Business Bureau to see what kind of record the facility has.

4. Visit the facility.

Interview the director and teachers. During this visit, you should:

■ Find out how many other children are in your child's class. (Younger children will require greater supervision, so while a class of five-year-olds with twenty-two students might be fine, a class of three-year-olds the same size would probably require two teachers or a teacher and an assistant.)

- Ask about accreditation. The facility may be accredited through the NAEYC (National Association for the Education of Young Children) or another organization. While lack of membership in no way lessens the value of the facility, belonging shows dedication and a desire to adhere to standards.
- Ask about academics. Is the day care primarily concerned with keeping the children safe and entertained, or is education a goal?
- Ask about teacher qualifications. At a very minimum, you should have teachers with high school diplomas and no felony convictions. An associate or bachelor's degree in child development, of course, would be desirable.
- Tour the facility. You should have free access to *all* classes, and you should find the staff alert and involved with the children. The staff should be warm and interesting, with spontaneous laughing, hugging, and eye-to-eye contact. The staff should be gentle but firm when necessary.
- Even if you don't have an infant, pay particular attention to the infant area. Observing how infants, who can't complain, are treated will give you an added insight into how the older children are treated. First off, infants need to be held and played with as well as kept fed and diapered. The infant area should *not* smell of urine and feces between diaper changes. And when diapers are changed, the person changing the diapers should wash the changing table *and* his hands before and after each change.

- Find out the policy on sick children. Normally, a day-care facility isn't allowed to admit a child who seems to be sick, unless a doctor or nurse gives approval in writing. This policy might occasionally create hardships for you, but it also protects your child from infectious disease.

- Make certain that you are always welcome for an *unannounced* visit. Make an unannounced visit from time to time, just to make certain that things run as well as expected when they're inspected.

- Be a part of the program. Your child *and* the school will appreciate your interest in their programs and development. Volunteer, whenever you can, to go along on field trips and to help out with a class or project. You, your child, and the center will benefit!

SUMMARY AND CONCLUSION

"The hand that rocks the cradle," William Ross Wallace wrote, "is the hand that rules the world." Today, the hand that rocks the cradle is often the hand of a professional day-care worker. When you choose those who will have your child to mold for forty or fifty or even sixty hours a week, make certain that they are kind hands, caring hands, competent hands. Also, make certain that the values and ideas that will be taught your child are the values and ideas that *you* would have taught your child, had you been able. Follow our guidelines and your own heart, hunches, and intuition, and you'll find a day-care center that suits your needs and your child's.

Chiropractor

OVERVIEW

In 1895, Daniel D. Palmer developed a principle and method of healing without drugs based on the belief that dysfunction is caused by the inhibition of nerve impulses flowing to different parts of the body. Palmer believed that manual manipulation of the spinal vertebrae allows nerve impulses to flow normally and, thereby, restores good health. He named the practice *chiropractic* from Greek words that mean "done by the hands."

Initially, Palmer's theory was condemned by medical doctors, but results obtained over the years eventually led to a grudging respect for the profession, and now many medical doctors refer patients to chiropractors. In 1993, the British Medical Association published *Complementary Medicine—New Approaches to Good Practice*, which supported official recognition of chiropractic, saying, "There is significant research on the effectiveness and safety of chiropractic . . . which now has a discreet and established education and research base, should practise [sic, British spelling] alongside orthodox medical care."

Until a few years ago, I was among the skeptics about chiropractic, considering it only slightly more advanced than the ancient witch doctor who wore a loincloth and danced and murmured chants while tossing incense and chicken feathers into the fire. However, I've since seen chiropractors help many people, even members of my own family, when "traditional medicine" had failed to bring relief. Therefore, I endorse the British Medical Association's high opinion of the profession.

However, since the quality of the schools and the length of training can vary, you'll need to check the tips and tactics before choosing a personal chiropractor.

TIPS AND TACTICS

1. Get recommendations.

Ask friends, and your medical doctor[9] for a list of qualified chiropractors in your area.

2. Check 'em out.

Call the Board of Chiropractors and the Better Business Bureau to see if any on your list have complaints filed against them.

3. Call the chiropractic office.

Tell them that you are looking for a chiropractor in your area and would like to ask some questions prior to making an appointment. Here are some questions to ask:

■ What school did the chiropractor attend? (Sherman College in South Carolina, we are told, is no longer accredited.)

■ Is the school the doctor attended accredited by the CCE (Council on Chiropractic Education)?

■ Did the school require at least three-and-a-third years to complete the degree requirements?

....

[9] Provided your medical doctor is a believer in chiropractic medicine. Unfortunately, some are not.

- Has the doctor done postgraduate work in some field (i.e., athletic, orthopedic, etc.)?

4. Visit the office.

The office should be clean, professional looking, and staffed by friendly, competent people.

5. Interview the doctor as he interviews you.

The doctor you choose should be one who asks intelligent questions and takes time to listen to your answers. In the same manner, he should be open to your questions and answer them simply and completely.

SUMMARY AND CONCLUSION

While today's chiropractors still adhere to Palmer's theory that dysfunction is caused by the inhibition of nerve impulses flowing to different parts of the body, they often use X rays along with standard physical and laboratory examinations to make a diagnosis and to prescribe treatment. Both the U.S. and Canada require graduates of chiropractic schools to pass an examination prior to obtaining a license. In neither country are chiropractors allowed to prescribe drugs.

Frankly, because of the differences in techniques and training, we have heard good and bad stories from people about chiropractic experiences. However, we have heard good and bad stories about physicians, dentists, and *all the other professions mentioned in this book*! Like any medical professionals, some chiropractors are more skilled than others. Therefore, use recommendations and your own good judgment in making a decision.

Chiropractors, by the way, were among the first in the medical field to become interested in the value of good nutrition to your health. In this area, they have led the AMA and the FDA. These groups have long been aware that small amounts of drugs ingested in your body could help, but they seemed unwilling to believe that the much larger quantities of foods we eat can affect our health— as long as we obtained our "minimum daily allowance" of vitamins and minerals. As Nobel prize-winning researcher Dr. Linus Pauling said, "*Minimum* means *minimum*—just that you won't die if you get that much. It *does not* mean that you'll be in optimal health with that amount!"

Because they believe so strongly in nutrition, many chiropractors will urge you to take vitamin, mineral, and even herbal supplements. Some sell these supplements themselves. If you trust your doctor, trust his or her recommendations. However, if you get good results from the vitamins and minerals your chiropractor sells you, you might check your local health-food store or vitamin wholesaler to see if you can obtain them for less money.

Computer Repairman

OVERVIEW

My idea for this book grew out of a computer problem I had in 1981. PCs were new then, and every manufacturer had its own DOS. Software that ran on one system usually didn't run on another. Consequently, whenever you had a problem, the hardware people said it was software related, and the software people said it was hardware related.

One day I had a problem, and began to call for help. Naturally, we played the old, familiar game. The hardware people said, "Software problem." The software people said, "Hardware problem." When I got them both on the line, they quickly agreed that it *must* be something *I* was doing wrong! Frustrated, I called the place that sold me the computer, talked to their computer expert, and packed the computer in my car and made the one-hundred-mile drive to Dallas.

When I arrived, I was able to demonstrate a set of perfectly legal keystrokes that precipitated a computer crash. My expert tinkered with it for a while, then scratched his head and said, "It's beyond me, I'll have to take it upstairs to my expert." I said, "I thought *you* were an expert!" He laughed and said, "Bockmon, every expert has an expert." Well, my expert's expert couldn't fix the computer, but *her* expert could! I learned three valuable lessons that day:

- Always know how to find an expert for the problems you can't solve.
- Every expert has an expert.
- A real expert doesn't mind referring you to *his* expert.

TIPS AND TACTICS

1. If it's under warranty, call the manufacturer or the place which sold it.

Note: this might not be the place you'll want to use if the item is out of warranty. I was out of town with my portable printer, and it quit working. I didn't have my warranty papers with me, but took it to a warranty repair place anyway. The repairman said that he would fix it and bill me, but if I found my warranty papers, they would cancel the bill. Fortunately, I found my warranty papers, because repairing the $280 printer cost $430!

2. Determine if the problem is hardware or software.

Strangely enough, I find most software has better field support than most hardware. I can buy an $80 piece of software and will find it's supported by a toll-free 800 number. A $2,700 printer has a toll number you can call, if you don't mind searching the fine print in the manual to find it. Then, should you need repair, they have a flat rate of $345 no matter how LARGE or small the problem. You don't want to take your unit in, only to find that the problem was a software glitch or a bad cable.

3. Ask your computing friends.

To have a computer (this is my *ninth)* is to have computer problems. Anyone who has used a computer for any length of time knows who to call for help. Ask your friends who they used. Ask if the PC came back fixed the *first time.* Ask if the charge was reasonable.

4. Look for someone certified.

The person working on your computer should have a degree in electronics or a technician's certificate.

5. Ask the repairman for references.

Even if a friend referred you to the repairman, ask for references. A friend once recommended her son-in-law as a computer repairman. He came out every Saturday for a long, long time, worked long, long hours, and told me what great discounts I was getting while giving me long, long invoices. Bit by bit (or should I say, "byte by byte"?), my bills added up to where they exceeded the cost of the unit! If I had checked the non-mother-in-law references, I'd have gone elsewhere in the first place.

6. Take the computer in.

Explain the problem in detail. Get a written estimate. Ask, "If this doesn't solve the problem, do I have to pay all charges or just for the work that finally fixes it?" (Chances are, you'll pay for everything, but it never hurts to ask, and at least you should get credit for any parts that don't fix the computer.)

7. Ask about warranty.

Ninety days on labor is standard. Some offer 120 days. Some parts are covered for longer periods.

8. Check it out before you leave.

I once made the mistake of buying a couple of computers from a bundler in Dallas. The units were supposed to be checked out, but they weren't. I drove a hundred miles to my office and neither computer worked. "No problem," the guy said, "just bring them back and we'll make them work." What the heck, it was only two hundred miles, round-trip. I brought them back, went to lunch, and when I got back to the store, they announced proudly that everything was, in their words, "All fix[sic]." I got back to my office and they still didn't work. "No problem—" the man began. I never got to hear what he might have said, because I assured him by this time it definitely *was* a problem. I made an *additional* two-hundred-mile round-trip into Dallas, went to lunch while they were "fix," and made them unpack them and prove that they worked before I left. (Strangely enough, they seemed irritated by my lack of trust!)

Always make certain it is working before you write the check and load the equipment.

SUMMARY AND CONCLUSION

People say Elvis was a bit strange because he would shoot his TV when Robert Goulet was on. At the time, I figured, "Hey, Elvis has lots of money, and the people who manufacture, transport, and sell TVs have to make a living, so why not? I mean, how often is Robert Goulet on? (I happen to like Robert Goulet, by the way.) I have never felt like shooting my TV, but I have often considered murdering my computer. If you use a computer, you know what I mean. You're right in the middle of the most complex document and you're thinking, Thank God, I'm almost through with this, and suddenly a box appears in the middle of your document and says something like: "Fatal error encountered." Isn't your first reaction to destroy the machine?

Getting the problem solved professionally may not be as emotionally satisfying as pumping a couple of .38 caliber bullets into the computer's electronic brain, but it is more cost-efficient. Therefore, before you resort to violence, take your computer to someone who can teach it some manners and respect. If you follow the preceding tips and tactics, you should have no difficulty finding a computer tamer.

Dentist

OVERVIEW

It is a noble profession, indeed, that works to reduce your need for their services. So it is with dentists, who for years have been pushing better dental hygiene and fluoridation of water to help reduce tooth decay, thereby reducing your chances of requiring expensive restorative dental care.

For a dentist, doctor, or any other degreed professional to graduate, they must meet *minimum* requirements. Naturally, most strive to perform far above the minimum. However, while you get to see diplomas, you don't get to see his report card from dental college, so you don't know if he was at the top, or the bottom, of his class. Therefore, you're going to have to get a report card from his *patients.* Here's how our dentist would go about rating a dentist he would use himself!

TIPS AND TACTICS

1. Don't rely solely on social contact.

Most of those interviewed said that the worst way to select a dentist is to pick someone simply because you've met him casually at a church, civic club, or other social function. Having these things in common might increase your comfort level, but it tells you nothing about his professional qualifications. Of course, if the dentist you've met socially passes the litmus test below, then by all means give friendship the edge.

2. Ask your friends.

Ask several people you trust to recommend a dentist they have used. Ask if they are satisfied with the quality of the work. Do they have to come back and have things redone?

Ask if their dentist emphasizes *prevention,* such as periodic X rays, cleanings, etc. These are low-profit items for a dentist, but good ones want to work with you to prevent problems as well as perform restorative work afterward.

If you ask ten friends and find one or more dentists appear more than once, begin your search there.

3. Call first.

Tell the receptionist you're looking for a dentist *and that you want to select one in advance of need.* Ask:

■ How long has the dentist been in practice? (One who just graduated from dental school will not be as experienced as a seasoned professional. One about to retire may not be there the next time you need him.)

■ How long has the dentist been in *this city?* (If a dentist moves around a lot, there may be a good reason!)

■ How many people work there? Is there a lot of turnover? (If a dentist can't keep employees, there might be a reason, too!)

■ Is the dentist a member of the Academy of General Dentistry?[10]

- Everyone is concerned about AIDS; what kind of infection control procedures do you use *to protect the patient*? (Instruments should be autoclaved after each use, gloves changed between patients, etc.)
- What do you charge for a routine office visit? A typical filling? Teeth cleaning? (There's nothing wrong with comparison shopping as long as you're comparing good dentists to good dentists. After all, it's not only your teeth and gums, it's your money.)

4. Case the joint.

Go in and look around. The office should be tasteful and restful. It should be clean, and the magazines should be fresh, current, and of general interest. (One dentist laughed and said, "If the books there are by Edgar Allen Poe or Stephen King, and the magazines are called *Masochist's Monthly* or *Sadists Review*, you might wish to look elsewhere!")

5. Case the dentist.

One dentist we interviewed said, "I wouldn't go to a fat dentist or one that wore thick glasses or trifocals, because they have to be able to get in close and see well to do their work."[11] This hurts, because the author could lose more than a few pounds himself—and wears (thin) bifocals. It also smacks of discrimination, but remember,

....

[10] Renewal of membership requires *continual* education, and you don't want a dentist whose formal education ended upon graduation!

[11] One of the dentists we interviewed dissented strongly with the previous statement, saying, "I disagree! If trifocals allow a person to see well and perform their job well, it should not be an issue. Worry when the dentist forgot his trifocals at home[sic]. I have known large dentists with a very delicate touch."

it is only *employers* and the government who cannot discriminate. *Consumers* can. In fact, being a "discriminating consumer" is considered a compliment. Decide for yourself whether the dentist just quoted had a good point and act accordingly.

6. What about franchise operations?

In recent years, franchise operations with dentists working on salary and/or a percentage of the profits have sprung up around the country. While the care provided by such places can be consistently high, sometimes young dentists start out in groups because they lack the funds to open their own offices. Therefore, your "favorite dentist" might or might not be there the next time you call. However, some experienced dentists like franchise operations because it allows them to practice dentistry without the additional stress of managing an office. Should you choose a franchise operation, be sure to ask about turnover, and how long *your dentist* has worked for the firm, and if he has announced plans to leave for private practice.

SUMMARY AND CONCLUSION

A good dentist should *listen* and be willing to discuss *alternative* courses of treatment. Good dentists *advise* and don't *sell*. A good dentist is open to your questions. If your dentist doesn't listen, won't answer questions, or won't discuss alternative courses of treatment, I'd call another dentist, explain the problem, and say, "I'd like to arrange an appointment and get a second opinion before I proceed."

Will a dentist resent your being proactive in your dental care? Some will. Most won't. Many people, myself included, tend to be a bit tense when we visit the dentist office. Even if we're going, as we should, for *preventive* dentistry, there's always a chance that they'll look inside your mouth and say, "Uh-oh!" Nothing eases tension like a warm, friendly, open, capable, caring dentist. You might never feel completely comfortable about dentistry, but if you take the time to check your options *before* you have a dental emergency, you can feel comfortable about your dentist.

Detective

On TV and in recent movies, detectives are called "private eyes" or "PIs," short for "private investigators." In older flicks, they were called "dicks" after Dick Tracy or "gumshoes" after the soft-soled shoes many wore so they could tail someone silently. Whatever the era, whatever the name, there has always been something alluring and mysterious about detectives. We remember Sherlock Holmes, Hercule Poirot, Nero Wolfe, Mike Hammer, Sam Spade, Miss Marple, Nick Charles, Ellery Queen, Magnum, Jessica Fletcher, Ace Ventura, and so on. In fiction, detectives are either detached (Holmes, Wolfe, Poirot, Marple) or tough, tenacious, and handy with their fists, guns, etc. (Spade, Hammer). *Just about all fictional detectives have a contact on the police force that can funnel them information that, while useless to the police, helps the detective solve the crime.*

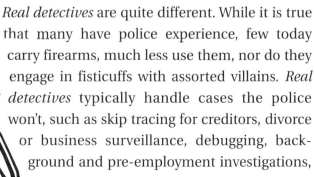

Real detectives are quite different. While it is true that many have police experience, few today carry firearms, much less use them, nor do they engage in fisticuffs with assorted villains. *Real detectives* typically handle cases the police won't, such as skip tracing for creditors, divorce or business surveillance, debugging, background and pre-employment investigations, finding children in custody battles, locating missing persons when there is no evidence of a crime, etc. A detective sells time and talent. It's the talent, of course, that makes his time valuable—and expensive, and some are more experienced—and expensive—than others. Here's how to find your own PI:

TIPS AND TACTICS

1. Ask around.

If you know an attorney, call and ask him to recommend some detectives with good reputations. Since some detectives were once police officers, some of our sources say that the detective division of your local police department is also a good source of leads, but other PIs disagree. If you can't, won't, or don't want to take this step, then check the Yellow Pages.

2. Check them out.

Detective agencies come and go. The one you want will have at least three or four years' PI experience. They should have a brochure, be able to provide you with references, and have nothing on their record at the Better Business Bureau. A call to the State Board of Private Investigators can also be revealing. Commit to nothing until you've checked them out.

3. Make certain they're up to date.

Today's investigator is familiar with electronic surveillance (and the laws governing its use) and probably has a computer on-line service such as ION (Investigation Operations Network) to provide a list of qualified detectives in other areas.

4. Meet with more than one.

If time permits, visit at least two agencies and explain what you need. Do not commit unless you feel comfortable with the agency and the agent.

5. State your needs clearly and concisely.

Tell the detective exactly what you want to accomplish and ask if he has the experience and resources to handle the case *and if he can provide references for similar work.* (If he doesn't, ask if he could recommend someone.)

6. Tell them everything pertaining to the case.

In fiction, the client always withholds vital information from the detective. This makes the detective's work more difficult, tense, and suspenseful. In *real life*, withholding information from your detective will also make his or her job *more expensive.* After all, you don't want to have to pay the detective to find out information you already know and could have provided for nothing!

7. Check prices.

Detectives usually charge by the hour and/or the day. If you get "ballpark" prices from several detectives, you'll get a feeling for what is reasonable.

8. Don't leave the "meter" running.

You do *not* want an open-ended agreement that allows you to continue to get bills but not results. Try to get an estimate for *the entire job,* and then agree to try it to an interim point for a lesser fee. This will give you a cap, and after you see whether or not the agency is likely to get the results you need, you can stop or go from there. Incidentally, most detectives charge less for a verbal report than

a written one—so you can save money if it's not important that your information be in writing.

9. Get someone flexible.

You want someone who will work with you and be ready
to go at a moment's notice. This is particularly important
in a surveillance job, where time is of the essence.

SUMMARY AND CONCLUSION

Joan Baez used to sing a plaintive lament that went,
"They're all putting in a *nickel*, and they want a *dollar*
song!" Naturally, we all want to save money, but buying a
detective isn't like buying an orange—they're not all the
same. A good detective might charge 20 percent more
than an average one, but might get results faster—making him less expensive than his lower-priced competitor.
Best bet: Go with the most experienced, most referenced
detective you can find for the money. Worst bet: Go with
someone you don't feel comfortable with, just because
he's cheap. (Remember, Neil Simon's play *The Cheap Detective* was a *comedy,* not a primer on what to look for!)

Doctor

OVERVIEW

Doctors stand between us and the ravages of accidents and disease. It takes talent, tenacity, training, and time to become a physician. Hippocrates (460-377 B.C.), the "father of modern medicine," was a talented internist and orthopedic physician. He taught his pupils to make a written record of patient symptoms, and patient and family history, and to accurately describe diseases and injuries. His own "field notes" are so detailed and precise that modern physicians can diagnose from them!

In addition to creating and codifying the profession, Hippocrates also brought a standard of ethics that comes down to us today as the Hippocratic oath. Students swore not only to try and heal, but to "do thy patient no harm." In addition, they were to lead their lives and practice in uprightness and honor, and respect a patient's confidences. A modified form of his oath is still administered by most medical schools today.

Avoid doctors who make you wait an hour to an hour and a half to see them. (Sometimes they attempt to fool you into thinking you're making progress by playing "musical rooms," a game in which you're eventually taken out of the waiting room to wait in a series of cubbyholes before the doctor appears.) Ironically, I have found that the physicians who make you wait the longest seem to be in the biggest hurry to get rid of you once you're there. You are an individual, and your health is too important for that kind of treatment. Doctors like that are only interested in "throughput," in putting patients through the system as rapidly as possible so they can make as much money as possible. Hippocrates would turn over in his grave!

Today, many people complain about the amount and quality of time their doctors spend with them. In an interview in *Parade* magazine,[12] former U.S. Surgeon General C. Everett Koop said, "If you talk to the people who receive health care, the number one concern is, 'My doctor is not the kind of man or woman I want a doctor to be. He doesn't listen to me.' Or, 'When I talk to her, she doesn't understand me.'"

Rude, rushed, rich doctors are a recent phenomenon that will only be erased when we patients refuse to stand for it. If we are half as discriminating in shopping for a physician as we are for other goods and services, we'll find a doctor who sees us as a person and not just a symptom, the kind of doctor our parents had and the kind many of us had growing up. Hippocrates was such a doctor. So are those we interviewed for this report. In fact, St. Luke, to whom we owe the Gospel of Luke, was such a caring doctor he was called the "beloved physician." Here's how to find *your* beloved physician.

....

[12] July 3, 1994

TIPS AND TACTICS

1. Find a family doctor first.

Dr. Koop believes that the first thing you do is find a good general practitioner, also known as a "primary-care physician." That is not an easy task. One reason is that the trend in the U.S. is to specialize, since specialists make more money. In the article previously quoted, Dr. Koop says, "In Britain, 72 percent of physicians are primary-care doctors. Canada has 54 percent. Germany and France have 47 and 48 percent. We have 29 percent, and the number is falling."

If you do a good job of finding a good primary-care physician, he will help you find specialists should the need arise. In fact, our sources tell us, "The best doctors do the most referrals."

2. Ask around.

Ask your friends, neighbors, insurance agent, and druggist who they use. If you've found the best hospital in the area, ask for a list of physicians who use the facility.

3. Call around.

Tell the receptionist that you are looking for a family doctor and would like to ask some questions. Ask your own, or these:

- How long has the doctor been in practice?
- How long has the doctor been in practice here?
- Is he planning to stay here? (You don't want to select a doctor who is about to move!)
- How old is the doctor? (*Employers* aren't allowed to discriminate on account of age, but individuals still

can. It does you little good to go through the selection process only to find your doctor is retiring in six months!)

What school did he graduate from, and what post-graduate work has he done?

What hospital or hospitals does he use? A study in Washington, D.C., and San Francisco, revealed that 50 percent of physicians use a single hospital for 95 percent of their cases, 30 percent use two hospitals, and less than 10 percent use four or more hospitals. I would feel more comfortable with a physician who used more than one facility, so he could match each hospital's specialty to my need.

■ Is he certified in his area of specialty? (If he's a general practitioner, he's probably a member of the American Academy of Family Practice.)

Does the office file insurance forms? (This is costly for the doctor but beneficial for you.)

■ Does the doctor take appointments?[13]

Do they notify you if the doctor is running late?

4. Look around.

Go into the offices of several doctors who pass your

....

[13] One physician we interviewed said, "I wouldn't go to a doctor that takes appointments, as most GPs deal with minor emergencies such as flu and colds. An appointment process denies timely access, and the patient might have to go to a minor emergency center and pay too much." Another physician said, "I wouldn't go to a doctor who *didn't* take appointments. A long wait indicates poor organization, possible patient overload, and possible inferior or hurried treatment." To me, when a doctor doesn't take appointments, he or she is saying, "*My* time is valuable, but *yours* isn't." *Cows* wait in line to see the vet, but then cows have a cud to chew and no pressing business that needs attending, nor do they have to pay their own medical bills. I don't want to be treated like a cow.

initial muster. Quietly take a seat in the waiting room and observe. You should find:

■ the room clean, but not opulent (If you find plush carpet and original objects of art, guess who is paying for it!)

■ the staff friendly, courteous, and cooperative with patients (Do not expect a good, caring doctor if the office is manned by a snarling, rude receptionist or nurse. A person good enough to manage your health should be good enough to manage employees.)

■ clean, neat magazines printed in your lifetime

5. Arrange an appointment.

If you have immunizations to be done, need a physical, or whatever, this is a good time to get it done and check out the doctor at the same time.

6. Allow yourself to be interviewed by the doctor.

On an initial visit this could take anywhere from fifteen to twenty minutes or more. During this period, you should have the doctor's *full attention*. Your physician should also be open to your questions. Your physician might not be a "beloved physician" like Dr. Luke in the Bible, but he should exude a caring attitude and a quiet confidence. If you don't feel comfortable with your physician when you're well, you certainly won't when you are ill!

7. Ask questions.

Ask questions about *tests*. In today's litigious society, it's common knowledge that many physicians order tests, not because they're needed for a diagnosis, but to protect themselves against a charge of not having exercised "due diligence" in providing health care. I'm not the suing kind, and I realize medicine is called a "*practice*" and not a "*perfect.*" Therefore, I see no reason to pay for tests designed solely or primarily to provide a parachute for my physician. Before I would begin any tests or treatments, I'd ask these questions:

Would you recommend these tests if insurance were not paying for them?

Are these tests designed to help you make a diagnosis, confirm one, or just for your own protection?

What success have you had with the treatment/drugs you're prescribing?

Is this the treatment you would prescribe for one of your own family members?

What is the projected time frame for this treatment to take effect?

8. Report your progress.

If physicians don't hear from you, they assume you got well or died. If you have not recovered at the end of your course of treatment, talk with the doctor about it, and ask what you should do next. Beware of a physician who:

can offer no explanation why the problems continue

doesn't suggest tests when the first treatment(s) fails

suggests that the symptoms are psychosomatic, yet doesn't refer you to a psychologist

says he's done all he can, yet doesn't refer you to a specialist

declines to refer you to another physician even when you ask him

SUMMARY AND CONCLUSION

My father once called me to tell me he was going in for surgery. Knowing this surgery was life changing, I asked if he'd gotten a second opinion. He replied, "No, but this doctor is well respected in his field." I asked, "Dad, if you took your car into an auto mechanic and he said it needed a complete engine overhaul, what would you do?" He thought a minute and said, "I'd take it someplace else and see what *they* said!"

I asked, "Would you do more for your car than you would for yourself?"

He got a second opinion, the physician elected to treat the problem with medication, and the problem went away. No surgery. No pain. No suffering. If memory serves, the medicine was fifty dollars. *The surgery was thousands of dollars.*

The point is, a good doctor will not only make referrals, he will urge you to get a second opinion if the course of treatment isn't working, or if his own diagnosis calls for drastic treatment. The fact that *not all* doctors do this merely points up the fact that we have to be *proactive* in our health care. We must not only answer questions our physicians put to us, we must ask them questions and, when necessary, question their answers.

Good health requires a partnership between doctor and patient. That partnership must be built on trust. They should be willing to invest the time to earn that trust, explain their diagnosis, their prognosis, and their course of treatment. We, on the other hand, should use our own brains, and if the treatment proposed is radical, life threatening, or expensive, we should insist on getting definitive answers to our questions and a second opinion.

When you go to get a second opinion, do not tell the second physician what the first physician said. Like lodge brothers, physicians have a difficult time contradicting one another. Just arrange to have your medical records sent over (They do belong to you, since you paid for them, no matter what the receptionist might try to tell you!) and ask, "What do *you* think?"

Davy Crockett said, "Be *sure* you're right, then go ahead." Before you allow your doctor to go ahead with painful, prolonged, expensive, life-threatening or life-changing treatment, be *sure he's right*—then go ahead! *Suggestion: Read the section under "How to Find an Expert: Hospital Staff."*

Druggist

Your druggist (or pharmacist) is a highly trained, respected member of your health team. As the *New Family Encyclopedia* puts it, pharmacology is a "branch of the healing arts which deals with the preparation, control, and distribution of medication." Pharmacists in the United States are trained at seventy-six accredited colleges, and the curriculum requires five years of study for a bachelor of science in pharmacy, six for a doctorate. Pharmacists are not only invaluable in dispensing drugs, but in advising doctors, dentists, and their patients about the effectiveness, side effects, and interactions of the drugs they dispense. Under federal law (OBRA 1990), pharmacists may offer to counsel you concerning medication. Some states, such as Texas, *require* a pharmacist to provide this counseling.

In addition to *offering* to counsel with you, your druggist—as dictated by federal law—may answer *your* health-care questions and either recommend an over-the-counter medication or suggest that you see a physician. (And if you ask *why* he thinks you should see a physician, he is required to tell you why.) These laws were written in recognition of the high degree of medical training pharmacists receive and to help relieve the workload on physicians. The bottom-line benefit to you is that you have a low-cost checkpoint when you're trying to decide if your health problem is something you can treat yourself or requires a greater degree of care.

All pharmacists are well educated and trained. Here's how to get one with the proper attitude.

TIPS AND TACTICS

1. Ask a health-care professional.
Your physician, dentist, or any of their nursing staff can provide you with a list of good pharmacists.

2. Call and ask to speak with the recommended pharmacist that sounds best.
Explain that you're looking for a pharmacist and would like to ask a few questions. Sample questions might include:

- How many years' experience do you have?(You don't want one that is too new or too near retirement. A pharmacist who has been in the business ten or twenty years can probably answer most of your questions without hesitation, because he's probably heard your question many times before.)

- What professional organizations do you belong to? (Membership in professional organizations shows that he is remaining active and continuing to learn.)

- Will you perform simple services such as cutting pills in half? (If you've ever tried this at home with a sharp knife, you know that you usually have to hunt for one end!)

■ Ask about possible drug interactions or side effects about a drug you *know about* from experience or from having looked it up in a copy of *Physicians' Desk Reference* at your local library. (You'll need to look elsewhere if the pharmacist says, "You'll have to talk with your doctor about that!" or "I can't give you that information.")

■ Do you accept insurance cards, and will you aid in insurance reimbursement?

3. Check pricing.

If you are currently taking a prescription medication, ask the pharmacist, "What do you charge for _____? How much do you charge for the generic (or brand-name, if you're taking the generic) version?" I wouldn't let price *alone* entice me to pick a pharmacist. However, all things being equal, you want to save money.

SUMMARY AND CONCLUSION

The trend in health care, from both a state and federal level, is to encourage consumers to rely more heavily on our highly trained pharmacists to relieve some of the pressure on physicians. Therefore, more than ever before, it is important that your pharmacist be a "people person," someone who will take time to explain drug side effects and interactions and to answer your health-care questions. While not a substitute for a physician, a good pharmacist can assist you in making the decision to treat a problem with "over-the-counter" medication or to seek the services of your primary-care doctor.

If the advice you get from your pharmacist doesn't seem right, check with another pharmacist or your physician. If your pharmacist treats you right, return the favor by recommending him to your friends. Conversely, should you find a pharmacist who is unable or unwilling to answer your questions, advise those who made the recommendation *and your physician.* Should you have serious problems, such as wrong medication, overcharging, or unauthorized substitution of a generic for a brand-name medication, you might wish to contact not only your physician, but your state board of pharmacy, as well.

Electrician

OVERVIEW

Unbelievable as it seems, not all states require electricians to be licensed. New York, for example, does; California *once did;* Texas never has. Some cities require licenses, but even that can vary. Some cities buy tests from an outside firm, and they're sealed in front of the person being tested and shipped off to be graded, thus guaranteeing that favoritism isn't a part of the process. Other cities prefer to develop their own tests. Some cities don't require any testing or credentials, but simply issue a license to anyone willing to pay the fee. Other cities don't require a license at all.

Even in areas where licenses *are* issued only after the candidate has exhibited a minimum standard of knowledge and gained a minimum amount of experience, some electricians are more skilled, more highly trained, more motivated, and more conscientious than others. Naturally, whether you're putting in another circuit, adding on to your home, or getting the wiring done for a new home under construction, you want the best you can find. Here's how you go about it!

TIPS AND TACTICS

1. Ask someone qualified to have an opinion.

This is one of the few areas where we *don't* suggest that you ask friends and neighbors. Call the following and ask for *a list of qualified electricians they can recommend.*

- your local electric utility
- your local electrical inspector
- a building contractor with a good reputation

2. Get the most qualified electrician available.

In some areas, there are electricians, journeyman electricians, and master electricians, with the master electrician having the most experience and knowledge. In other areas, these are merely titles that electricians like to use. Ask your local electrical inspector what's true in your state.

3. Drive by the electrician's place of business.

Customers pay for elegant offices, so you're not looking for an office that's opulent and fancy, but you do want an electrician who has roots in the community, with more going for him than a mobile phone and a pickup truck.

4. Call the most likely candidate.

Answering machines (or "voice mail," as it's known in larger firms) are wonderful. They take down every word of your message so someone can get back to you. However, when you call and get an answering machine during business hours, you don't know if the person you want is just down the hall or if the only person on staff is out on a job. You want an electrician that will be there whenever you need him, so it's reasonable to expect that a human will answer the telephone during normal office hours.

Also, ask what and how he charges. Some electricians charge from the time they leave their office (or their last job!) until they get to your place. If their last job was across the county, that could add up. When it comes to billing, the best surprise is no surprise. (I wouldn't want you to be "shocked" by your bill!)

5. Ask for references.

A qualified practitioner, whatever the profession, doesn't mind giving references. References, of course, are meaningless unless you check them.

6. Ask if he's bonded and insured.

An electrical mistake could conceivably cost you your home. You want an electrician who is bonded and has liability insurance for any damage he might do or injuries his workers might suffer.

7. Ask if he provides after-hour service.

When I had an electrical problem, at night, and on the weekend, I called the electric company, and they were hesitant to give an individual recommendation. Finally I said, "Look, I've got a freezer full of food, writing deadlines are flying like Frisbees on the first day of spring. If *you* had to call an electrician, who would you call?" He gave me the name of R. G. Good. Mr. Good, who was a master electrician in a state where the title had to be earned, had never heard of me, but he came out, dug up the electrical line, and repaired it. He *charged me the same as he would have for day service!* I had expected (and insisted on) paying extra for this extra service, but the point is, he came out. If your electrician won't come whenever you need him, then you need to look for one who will.

8. Your electrician should be able to communicate.
He should be able to explain just what he is going to do, why, and what it will cost.

9. Avoid an electrician who suggests cutting corners.
Electricity is a safe source of energy, but codes and rules are written for reasons. Avoid anyone who suggests you violate a state or local code, or take shortcuts.

SUMMARY AND CONCLUSION

We were shocked to find that so many areas do not have licensing requirements for something as important as electrical work. Texas licenses beauty operators in spite of the fact that no one has ever died from a bad haircut, but doesn't license electricians whose mistakes can cause major disasters. However, by carefully checking with those most in the know about qualified electricians and by taking a bit of your own time to investigate, you should find an electrician who can do a good job at a fair price.

Electronic/TV Repairman

OVERVIEW

If you're thinking all it takes to be in the electronic repair business is a sign that says, "Electronic Repair," well, you're absolutely right—in many places. In the days of vacuum tubes, most electronic "repair" was simply tube replacement. Today's electronics rely on solid state components soldered into PCBs or PWBs (Printed Circuit Boards/Printed Wiring Boards), and are comparatively trouble free. When a component *does* go out, however, it requires sophisticated electronic equipment, *and* a high degree of skill and training to track down and repair the problem.

In the old days, the electronic repairman's biggest competitor was the tube-testing machine at the local convenience store. Today, his biggest competition on electronic repair of items under two hundred dollars is the local discount store! That's because it takes a lot more time and skill to repair an item than it does to assemble it—and most assembly is done in countries where employers don't face the burden of American wages, taxes, and worker benefits.

Still, it makes sense to at least consider the cost of more expensive items and, naturally, anything that has sentimental value. (Antique radios and TVs requiring vacuum tubes can still be repaired, because some companies manufacture modern components to fit in the old tube sockets!)

TIPS AND TACTICS

1. Shop for a replacement.

Electronics, for a variety of reasons, tend to become less expensive as time goes by. Chances are, you will find replacement units, with more features than yours, that cost less than you paid for the old unit. For the basis of comparison, however, determine the cost of the item *most like your current unit.* Do not buy a replacement at this time, but keep a mental note of the cost.

2. Get recommendations.

Ask friends, neighbors, and co-workers if they've had anything electronic repaired lately, and if it was done cost effectively and correctly the first time.

3. Call and ask to speak to one of the technicians.

Tell him what your item is and what is wrong with it.

■ If the unit is inexpensive, say, "This unit is about __ years old, and I know that I can get a new one at _____ for about $_____. Do you think this item is worth repairing?" If you receive a "no" answer, go directly to the store where you found the similar item and replace it. If you receive a "yes" answer, go directly to step four.

4. Get some credentials.

Ask what kind of experience they have. I would feel comfortable if told:

- I have three or more years' military electronic experience or in an electronics lab.
- I have a degree in electronics.
- I'm a member of ISCET (International Society of Certified Electronic Technicians), which is a requirement in some states.
- We're the factory-authorized repair center for that brand. (Factory-authorized repair centers will usually have well-trained technicians who are checked out on the entire line. In addition, should they have a question, they have a hotline to the factory. However, factory-authorized repair places *might* be more expensive. (Read the "Computer Repair" section for a cautionary note on factory-authorized repair.)
- I have five (or more) years of experience in electronic repair.

5. Ask about estimates.

Some places will give you a free estimate. Most often, you'll be asked to pay a set, nonrefundable fee for diagnosing your problem. (However, some shops will apply the fee to the cost of repair if they do the work, which is reasonable.) If you're paying for diagnostics, it should be in writing with an estimate for the repair. This will enable you to competitively check prices.

6. Check it out.

Go to the repair place and look around. A well-maintained, neat place inspires confidence, but electronic repair places are notoriously junky, and I've seen some fine work come out of places that looked like they had been vandalized. I would be suspicious, however, if I saw a bunch of old, dusty TVs, VCRs, and stereos sitting around waiting to be picked up, because it could mean the owners had been hit with a bigger bill than expected.

SUMMARY AND CONCLUSION

When one of the last remaining TV assembly plants in the United States closed, management praised the workers at the plant, but explained that the cost of labor at the American plant was just under thirteen dollars an hour, while at the new plant in Mexico it was less than two dollars an hour. He went on to explain that, with global competition for TV sets, the American plant couldn't be competitive with an eleven-dollar-an-hour wage differential.

Most of the repair shops we talked to charge from forty to sixty dollars an hour. The charges are reasonable, because as we said earlier, it takes more time, talent, and training to track down and repair a problem than it does to solder or screw in a component on a factory line. But the fact remains that it doesn't take too many hours of expensive labor to exceed the entire cost of manufacturing and assembling the article in a third-world country. Therefore, unless the item has sentimental value, I wouldn't consider repairing anything that could be replaced for less than ninety minutes' shop labor.

Estate Appraiser

OVERVIEW

There's an American proverb that goes, "When someone says, 'It's not the *money*, it's the *principle*,'—it's the *money!*" A few years ago, I had an opportunity to witness how quickly *grieving* turns into "*greeding*." Arguments about who is to inherit what can happen in the best, most closely knit families. Today, with so many blended families sharing an inheritance, arguments are often the norm.

In this particular case, two middle-aged people who had lost spouses married. Each had grown children, and one of the husband's daughters had been best friends with the wife's daughter long before their widowed parents had met. First the husband died, then the wife. At the death of the wife, her children immediately began disbursing the estate. They not only presented a united front against their stepfather's children, but soon began squabbling among themselves. This would have been bad enough under any circumstances, but there weren't millions or even tens of thousands of dollars involved. The paltry nitpicking arguments were over an estate that, if properly divided, would have only amounted to a few hundred dollars per child. The natural children of the father decided that the squabble wasn't worth the damage to the memories and left it to the others. Yet, fellowship and a best friendship were broken.

Even in the best of families, several people can be expected to come forward and say, "Aunt Bea wanted me to have these!" It is not always greed and avarice, or money and mendacity that cause this. Sometimes, there is an honest difference of opinion as to what Aunt Bea said, or meant to say. And sometimes, the Aunt Bea's of the world forget and promise the same thing to more than one relative! Yet, as families go down the list of items, it becomes very easy for one to start attributing wrong motives to the other, and arguments and hurt feelings ensue.

An equitable division of property requires that everyone know what each item is worth. You accomplish this by having the estate appraised. With an appraisal in hand, property can be sold, or family members can take turns selecting items of similar value. It is not only more fair, it is easier on the soul and kinder to the memory of the one whose property is being distributed. Often, the appraisal reveals that some of the *least regarded* items are among the more valuable!

Your appraisal, of course, should be for the *wholesale* value of the items, and you should bear in mind that whoever sells the items will earn a commission. Also, if they are sold at auction, certain items might bring much more or much less than the item is actually worth. However, a good appraiser will look at everything with a practiced, seasoned, experienced, *unemotional* eye and will be able to say, "While Aunt Bea's china might be worth thousands to you because of the sentimental value, on the open market it'll only bring $350." Or, "That little painting that none of you liked is really the only valuable piece of art in the collection. A similar work by the same artist brought twenty thousand dollars at a recent auction!"

Now that you know *why* you need an estate appraiser, let's look at how you go about finding one.

TIPS AND TACTICS

1. Do not attempt to separate the junk from the treasures.

There's a natural tendency to dump the stuff in the drawers, trash the gift item bought at Graceland or the old broken rocker. But gum wrappers have sold for fifty dollars, a single marble for ten thousand! It is true that "one man's trash is another man's treasure," and the things you might toss out could well be the very thing a collector would pay dearly to own!

Old photographs, stamps, antique firearms, even the circa fifties school lunch box might be very valuable. Let the appraiser see everything before you distribute or discard anything.

2. Make a list of likely candidates.

Before you talk to any appraiser, generate a list to work from to help you decide. Call the American Society of Appraisers[14] and ask for certified appraisers in your area. If you have a special area of interest, i.e., stamp or coin collection, you might ask, "Who specializes in these?"

■ Check *Antiquities* magazine for lists of experts in your area.

■ Call antique dealers in the area, and ask them for suggestions. It is possible, even likely, that many of these dealers also do appraisals. If so, say, "Then I'll certainly want to talk with you, but right now, I'm trying to get a *list* to see who would be the best one to contact. What is *your particular area of expertise?*" Then, proceed as outlined in the subsequent steps.

3. Match expertise to the estate.

In the front of the book we quoted Will Rogers's classic line, "Everybody is ignorant, just on different subjects." Many appraisers are *generalists*, much like a medical doctor that is a general practitioner. However, if you have paintings, fine jewelry, oriental carpets, art glass, firearms, etc., you'll probably require an appraiser who specializes in those. If you have both general and specialty items, advise the appraisers you interview and ask if they can recommend someone for the special items. (These "someones" must be subjected to the same qualification process as your primary appraiser!)

4. Ask for references.

Naturally, you'll want references from clients he has represented who had merchandise similar to yours.

....

[14] One appraiser we spoke with took exception to this, saying that membership is a hundred dollars a month and it's not necessary to belong to be a good appraiser. Whether or not you agree, it is *one* of the places you could start your search for likely candidates. However, one valid benefit of associations is that they provide networking to help an appraiser check values of items he might not be familiar with.

References, naturally, are of no value to you unless you check them.

5. Ask if he is bonded.

It's a reasonable question and one that a qualified estate appraiser has been asked many times before. Should something go wrong, you will be glad you got an affirmative answer before entrusting your treasures to his care.

6. Negotiate fees in advance.

You might be quoted a flat fee, a percentage, or an hourly figure. Look for someone who charges by the hour. It gives them fair compensation for their time, saves you money if the appraisal doesn't take as long as they thought, and helps curb any temptation to raise the evaluation in order to raise the fee. *If the appraiser is also going to sell the merchandise for you, negotiate the fee for that, in writing, at the same time.*

SUMMARY AND CONCLUSION

Any business transaction, large or small, requires an element of trust. Since many people and many emotions are usually involved in settling an estate, it is important that there be a great deal of trust between you and the appraiser(s) you select to assist you. Throughout the process, you should feel comfortable with your appraiser. He should answer your questions frankly, and when he doesn't know the answer, he should admit that, too.

Before you sign anything, you need to go to the appraiser's place of business. A good appraiser should have a large selection of reference books. Moreover, he should be willing to share them with you whenever you question the value of a certain item. The appraiser should be willing to communicate with you on how individual items were priced. Beware of an appraiser who is evasive, wary, indirect, claims to be an expert in every field, or who offers to buy an item he has appraised.

Remember, if you negotiated properly, you are paying your expert by the hour. Cut the meter off and cut them a check for services rendered to date if you begin to get uneasy. If you have doubts, call another appraiser and get a second opinion for the items that have already been appraised. While there will naturally be differences of opinion, the overall total should be very close.

Family Counselor

OVERVIEW

When we need counsel and advice, there are many places we can go. Most often, we turn to friends. If our needs are deeper or more private, we might seek the counsel of a minister, priest, or rabbi. There are times, however, when we might require the counsel of someone who has been intensively trained in counseling. This might be a psychologist or a psychiatrist.

A psychologist is one who has at least a bachelor's degree in psychology. Those who plan to become clinical psychologists usually serve a year's internship at a psychological clinic, where they work under the supervision of experienced therapists. A Ph.D. in psychology requires four additional years of study.

A psychiatrist is a medical doctor who has also had three years of study in treating mental illness. As a physician, a psychiatrist can prescribe drugs. In this section,  we shall deal with family counselors, who are psychologists. Should your counselor feel that your problem requires a psychiatrist, he will refer you to one in your area.

There are a dozen major fields in psychology. Family counselors frequently specialize in *clinical psychology*, a field designed to help individuals better cope with the problems of daily life. Here's how to find a qualified practitioner in your area.

TIPS AND TACTICS

1. Get referrals from professionals you trust.

A doctor, a minister, or a friend who is in or has successfully completed counseling are good sources. You can also call the American Psychological Association, the American Association for Marriage and Family Therapy, or the American Counseling Association, and ask for accredited members in your area.

2. Make certain that your family counselor is accredited.

If you didn't get a referral from one of the organizations just mentioned, you'll want to check anyone who makes your "short list of prospects" to make certain they are all they appear to be. Unfortunately, in most states, anybody can run an ad offering "family counseling." Picking a counselor at random is like picking a puppy of unknown ancestry from a large litter. There is no way of telling what you'll wind up with! The family counselor you want will:

- be licensed by your state as a counselor
- have a degree *from a reputable college or university* relating to his field
- belong to organizations such as the American Psychological Association, American Association for Marriage and Family Therapy, the American Counseling Association, etc.

Licensing requirements vary from state to state. In Texas, for example, up until 1993, anyone could call himself a counselor. On January 1, 1994, it became a misdemeanor to practice counseling without a license. Licensing requires at least a bachelor's degree in psychology from an accredited college or university. In California, in addition to the aforementioned credentials, licensing also requires that the counselor complete at least six months of personal psychotherapy.

3. Call and chat with the counselor.

Explain what your problem is and what you hope to get from counseling. Then ask questions such as these:

- Have you done your own personal psychotherapy?[15] (A counselor who has not done his own work might have trouble keeping his own feelings and issues out of your therapy.)

- Can you tell me about your style and your theory of how change occurs?

- What kind of time lines are typically involved? How long does this kind of therapy usually take?

- What kind of success have you had working with others with similar problems?

- Have *you* ever had problems along the same line?[16] Have you successfully dealt with them?

- What are your fees per session? Does (name of your

....

[15] One counselor, who wished to remain anonymous, said she felt this question was inappropriate and irrelevant. However, others and the state of California feel differently.

[16] The same anonymous counselor who took exception to the question about the counselor's personal therapy had the same comments on this question.

insurance company) usually cover this? (In 1994, we are told that fees in Texas range from twenty-five dollars up per session for a counselor with a bachelor's degree, from sixty dollars up for a counselor with a master's, and eighty dollars and up for a counselor with a Ph.D.)

4. Schedule an office visit.

Your first session will probably be primarily devoted to getting acquainted. During this visit, you should:

- feel comfortable with your counselor
- see evidences of diplomas, reference books, etc.
- find that your counselor is very open to your questions
- establish a time line for evaluating the therapy (In other words, if you aren't getting better by a certain time, you both need to agree to a referral.)

SUMMARY AND CONCLUSION

Years ago, when our daughter was going through the throes of adolescence, I asked her, "Rebecca, which is easier: to decide what you ought to do or what someone else ought to do?" She thought a moment and replied, "To decide what someone else ought to do, of course." I nodded and said, "I agree. So figuring you might be having trouble deciding what to do, here's what *I* think!"

I don't want to create the impression that my brilliant setup with my daughter got me anywhere. But the point is, it is often easier for someone not emotionally involved in the issues to see them more clearly. This is true of anyone, but it is especially true when the outsider has received years of specialized training and has years of experience.

I believe in counseling. I once wrote a book with a counselor, and counseling has helped strengthen my marriage and family relationships. It can do the same for you, if you take the time to find the right counselor.

Fencing Contractor

Fencing is one of those things that looks easy . . . until
you decide to do it. I have personally built chain-link
fences, wooden fences, and barbed-wire fences. If you
haven't done any of these things, you're probably not as
likely to call a fencing contractor as I am—because it isn't
easy. Building a fence is a lot of hard work. Building a
fence that *looks good* is not only hard work, but it takes a
lot of time, talent, and patience.

Before you start thinking about your contractor, you
need to start thinking about your materials. The two
most common types of home fence are chain link
(woven wire) and wood. Let's look at each:

■ *CHAIN LINK*

Not all chain-link fencing is the same. Gauges differ,
and the better stuff is galvanized *after* it's woven. Also,
the size of tubing can vary. A dozen years ago, I decided
to build a chain-link dog run and discovered that a national catalog chain sold top rails, line posts, end posts,
and gates for less than the local building supplier. When
the materials arrived, I discovered that the material was
not only thinner, but smaller in diameter, than those I'd
seen at the local building supplier! While the material
was sturdy enough to contain a fourteen-pound
poodle, it wouldn't have been sufficient for the rough

and tumble play of my fourteen-year-old son. I spent a bit less money, but I got a whole lot less quality. When you discuss the cost of materials with your contractor, be sure you're comparing apples to apples and not apples to apricots. Tubing should have 0.055 wall thickness, and the fabric should be true twelve-gauge, and be double dipped and galvanized after weaving. Posts should be two-and-three-eighths-inch SS20 steel, and depending on soil conditions, should be set about one and one-half feet into the ground, with the top of the post lined up with your top rail.

■ *WOOD*

Wooden fences also differ, and the differences go far beyond whether you want a straight, round, gambrel, or dog-ear pattern at the top. A few years ago, I told a contractor I wanted to replace my four-foot cedar fence. I discovered he was pricing not cedar but something he called "white wood." (Don't bother checking your *Field Guide to Trees and Shrubs,* as "white wood" isn't listed.) The cost of constructing your fence will be about the same regardless of the wood you use, but some woods last longer (and are more expensive) than others. Among untreated woods, redwood and cedar last longest. However, common pine when treated with a process called Wolmanizing is guaranteed for thirty years *in the ground.* (The process makes the wood much heavier, however, and your fence will require extra support, and it might warp in some climates.)

Whatever wood you use for your fence, posts should go *deeply* into the ground, at least a foot and a half, more if you have a sandy soil. A deeply set post will provide strength to help your fence endure the winds of time. Posts should also be treated against water and insects. Galvanized metal posts can be used for chain-link or wood fences, offer good resistance to water, and are impervious to insects. Metal posts, of course, should be set in concrete, while wood posts should never be.

Besides water and insects, the greatest threat to the life of your fence is wind. Strong winds, or even moderate winds over time, loosen boards, cross pieces, and even posts. One way to minimize wind erosion is to build a staggered fence, with every other board being on the opposite side of the rail. This provides slightly less privacy, but allows the wind to pass without weakening your fence.

Whatever style of boards you use, be sure to use aluminum or galvanized nails. Ordinary nails will rust, leaving dark brown streaks down the face of each board.

This concludes your fencing primer. We now proceed to how to find a good fencing contractor!

TIPS AND TACTICS

1. Check around.

Ask neighbors who have had their fences for several years who they used. Or drive by a neighborhood that's a few years old, check the condition of the fences, and note the names on the contractor tags. Then call the Better Business Bureau and check for any complaints. Since home builders contract for a lot of fencing, you might also call your local or national home builders' association for recommendations. However, builders of new homes offer a one-year warranty, and some builders will go with the cheapest fencing contractor they can find, who in turn might not necessarily be the best fencing contractor or use the best materials. (See the section titled, "How to Find an Expert: Building Contractor.")

2. Call the leading contenders.

Tell them approximately how many feet of fence you need and what kind of fence you want. (Example: I want a four-foot cedar fence with one three-foot and one four-foot gate. I want treated metal posts sunk in concrete.) Ask them:

- How long have you been in business? (Take anyone new at your own risk.)
- Could you come out, do an estimate, and bring both a list of references and some samples of the materials you'll be using?
- How long do you warranty the workmanship and materials? (A year is fairly standard.)

3. Make certain that the estimate covers everything.

Never assume anything. Make certain that the price you get is the complete price, including gate hardware and taxes, and that the estimate affirms as much.

4. *Pass on anyone who:*

- says you have to pay in advance
- applies pressure
- seems shifty or evasive
- doesn't seem to have the tools or knowledge to do the work
- comes to your door uninvited (A magnetic sign and a pickup truck do not a fencing contractor make. Don't join the list of folks who paid a stranger in advance for work that was never done.)

5. *Investigate.*

Never make a decision on the spot. Take time to check the references.

SUMMARY AND CONCLUSION

In many areas, you need a permit to put up a fence, although no permit or license is required to be a fencing contractor. That means that there are no mandatory training or construction standards. Therefore, you should make certain that you feel very, very comfortable with a fencing contractor before he becomes *your* fencing contractor.

Again, never pay in advance. Most contractors I've talked with are happy to be paid upon *successful* completion of the project. The most I'd put up front would be one-third, payable upon delivery of *all* the fencing materials. Be cautious of contractors who ask for too much up front. After all, they have a lot less to lose than you do.

The contractor's trucks have wheels, and an unscrupulous one could be in the next state by morning. Your home, on the other hand, is going to stay put and will remain easy for the contractor to find.

Having said all that, it is my experience that, while talents and quality of workmanship vary, most people in the fencing business are honest. Still, be careful in selecting a contractor, check prices, and enjoy your new fence.

Financial Planner

OVERVIEW

"Financial planning" is a term often thrown around loosely, because there is no set definition of a financial planner. The term can be used by anyone who helps someone else make a "financial plan." By this loose definition, any parent who helps an adolescent child budget his allowance is a "financial planner." (It's rather difficult to persuade children to *pay* for your advice, however!)

In the adult world, most folks calling themselves "financial planners" have something to sell—sometimes only *one* something,[17] usually an insurance program, but sometimes precious metals, commodities—even real estate. There is nothing wrong with any of these items, but salespeople tend to sell what they know best. As the adage goes, "When you're a hammer, everything looks like a nail!" Anyone who really believes in his product might be biased toward it. Therefore, if all your financial planner primarily sells is _____(fill in the blank yourself), don't be surprised to discover that his financial plan will include lots of _____ (copy in the word you wrote in the first blank).

....

[17] There's nothing wrong with selling. It's a valuable, honorable profession. In fact, I co-authored a book called *Samurai Selling* (St. Martin's Press, 1993) that teaches how to sell through service.

However, experienced financial planners are knowledgeable about and can offer investments advice in several fields: stocks, bonds, tax-exempt securities, mutual funds, annuities, CDs, precious metals, IRAs, commodities, or what-have-you. Some might sell some or all of these themselves; others might sell one or two and refer you to another expert for the balance. The important thing you want from a financial planner is a recommendation of *what you need* and not just *what they have to sell.*

A financial planner will use various tools to help you manage cash, set goals, accumulate wealth, plan retirement, manage risk (through insurance and buying strategies), pick investments, and obtain quick cash when you need it. Sound like advice you need? Here's how to find yours!

TIPS AND TACTICS

1. Get referrals.
The referrals need to come from professionals you admire and respect, such as your attorney, banker, or CPA.
2. Get credentials.
In the insurance field, the credential that means the most is CLU (Chartered Life Underwriter). Also look for ChFC (Chartered Financial Consultant) and CFP (Certified Financial Planner) certification. CFPs are certified by the College of Financial Planning in Denver, Colorado. The CLU and ChFC certification are obtained through the American College out of Bryn Mawr, Pennsylvania.

3. Ask if they give a complimentary first interview.

If so, interview the financial planner and allow him to interview you. During this meeting, he will find out a lot about you and your financial position and goals. In addition, you should find out a lot about him, leaving not only with the knowledge you need, but with the feeling that he is evaluating your situation objectively, not just selling you what he has to offer. Here are some questions you might wish to ask to help you decide:

- How do you charge? Fees? Commissions? Fees and commissions? (We found a one-time fee range of one hundred seventy-five to thirty thousand dollars, depending on the complexity of the plan. The average was around five hundred dollars.)
- What financial products do you personally sell? How do you keep yourself from becoming overly biased about a product?
- Can you give me references? (Remember, unchecked references are no better than no references at all.)
- Can you show me a sample financial plan to give me an idea of your work?
- How long have you been in this business? (Four or five years is a good starting place.)

4. Check credentials.

Call the International Association of Financial Planners to see if the person is registered. Call the references he gave you, and ask them how long they've had the financial planner and if they are satisfied with his performance.

SUMMARY AND CONCLUSION

Do not confuse *financial* planning with *estate* planning. Estate planning is an entirely different arena, and you'll want an estate planner, perhaps even a board-certified estate planner, to work with you, your attorney, your CPA, or a CLU to plan for the protection and distribution of your estate.

Above all, take time to learn what your financial planner does and why he does it. Never give anyone else unquestioned, unauthorized control over your money or your investments. We invest to provide security, but as they used to say at the Strategic Air Command, "Eternal vigilance is the price of security." Be vigilant.

Mark Skousen, who holds a Ph.D. in economics, served as economics officer for the CIA, and edits an investment newsletter, says the best way to protect your assets from those who want to uncover, expose, or otherwise threaten your wealth is to "never let one person, especially a financial planner, know everything about your affairs." In other words, Mark is saying, "Don't tell anyone more than they need to know."

As a rule of thumb, I would be in favor of full disclosure to my financial planner. However, if for some reason you, like Mark Skousen, wish to shield knowledge of some of your portfolio, then tell your planner that, while you have other investments, you want him to handle the remaining portion as if that were all there was. Still, keep in

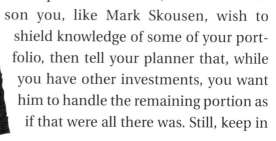

mind that you're asking your financial planner to work partly in the dark.

While some have more dollars to gain or lose than others, we can all lose all we have. Therefore *every financial plan* is important. Take the time to find the right planner.

Funeral Director

OVERVIEW

Ben Franklin said, "In this world, nothing is certain but death and taxes." In other sections of this book, we've dealt with taxes. Now we turn our attention to death.

Scripture says, "It is appointed to man once to die, and then the judgment." Shakespeare wrote, "It seems to me most strange that men should fear; seeing that death, a necessary end, will come when it will come." Death will come to all of us, and since laws and customs prohibit placing bodies on the curb in a Hefty bag, our final remains must be given a final resting place.

Burial customs vary from place to place and from time to time. In ancient Egypt, the very wealthy were embalmed with such consummate skill that many are still remarkably well preserved even today. Pharaohs, who had unlimited wealth and manpower, began planning for their death and burial from the very beginnings of their reign. And although the monuments of their self-glory are impressive even after the passage of centuries, one can't help but feel sad to know that these men lived their entire lives with their death foremost in their mind!

With the exception of the wealthy and powerful, for most of recorded history, death was handled matter-of-factly as it came. Burial arrangements were simple, family affairs. Consequently, when someone died, the body was washed, dressed, and placed in a simple coffin or blanket, while other friends dug the grave. The deceased was then interred in the earth, and friends and family celebrated the life just gone and the life to come.

In earlier times, cemeteries were often adjacent to churches. There was something comforting about knowing that the older members are still with the church, waiting in the grass for the arrival of the members who are still meeting inside, confident in faith that eventually they will all meet again and worship together in new life and with the same spirit. Even as a child, I enjoyed wandering through older cemeteries, marveling at the variety of headstones, and at the last words of wisdom—and often wit—that were carved there.

When we build churches today, we don't include land for cemeteries. Cemeteries are run as a business, many as *incorporated* businesses. This can be good, as paid maintenance is often more reliable than volunteer maintenance. In fact, the descriptive phrase for many of today's cemeteries is "perpetual care." In order to provide perpetual care, they eschew those old, ornate, distinctive, and hard-to-trim-around upright headstones so the lawn mowers and weed eaters can get in and do their work. Today's "headstone" is apt to be a bronze plaque lying flat on the ground, frequently with a small bronze vase attached into which kith and kin place plastic flowers.

One day, as my wife and I were heading from Austin to Georgetown on Interstate 35, I looked over and saw one of those large, incorporated cemeteries, flat as a pan-cake. You couldn't see the flat bronze plaques marking final resting places from the road, but I knew they were there—because there were acres and acres of plastic flowers sticking out of the little bronze urns. And I turned to my wife and said, "I've finally decided what I want to put on my tombstone: *'Thank you for not placing plastic flowers on this grave!'* "

The simple blankets, the rude unfinished coffins of yesterday are replaced today by well-oiled, well-polished caskets. These pieces of furniture are finer and more expensive than most of the occupants ever owned in life. Items of this quality aren't made by neighbors with basic carpentry skills, but by artisans in factories. Instead of a neighbor washing the body and dressing him in the "best suit" or her in the "best dress," morticians embalm the body. Cosmeticians and beauticians provide makeup and hairstyling. Dresses and suits can be bought "off the rack" at the funeral home, and professionals not only assist in the purchase of a stately casket, but often a burial vault (lest the body eventually come into contact with the earth from which it came[18]), mausoleum space, flowers, music, rental cars, etc. They even help us with the paperwork required to prove to our government that a taxpayer has, at last, slipped beyond their grasp. In certain other countries, if the deceased was unknown or unpopular, professional mourners can also be hired for the occasion.

---

[18] Concrete liners are sometimes required by cemeteries.

The old-fashioned way of handling death was certainly more intimate and less expensive, but who is to say it was better? Just as our culture once accepted the family funeral service as the norm and even those who might have been a bit squeamish about it went along, so today our culture accepts the idea of turning the whole sad affair over to professionals. Even those who might prefer otherwise are a bit squeamish about bucking the tide of fashion.

There's no denying that funeral directors earn their keep. It's a tough job because they deal with grief and sadness on the part of the mourners—and firsthand grief, even the grief of a stranger, is hard to bear. If their prices seem a bit high, and if their stilted language seems a bit strange (One somberly suggested that I might prefer a certain casket for my mother because, "It has an adjustable back for more comfortable reposing."), the service they provide is something most of us wouldn't do for twice the money.

Here's how to find a funeral director that will meet your needs.

TIPS AND TACTICS

1. Ask those who've recently dealt with death.
Ask your minister, priest, or rabbi for a recommendation. Either that, or call someone who handled a funeral you attended where you thought things went tastefully and smoothly.

2. Visit the funeral home.

On your tour, you should note:

- the general appearance of the facility (Does it suit your taste?)
- the appearance and attitude of the staff (Under the circumstances, do you feel reasonably comfortable with them?)
- if the service is to be held on the premises (Is there adequate room inside, plenty of parking, etc.?)
- if they listen to you, and are attentive and sympathetic to your needs (After all, they should be willing to plan the service as *you* want it, not try to dissuade you by saying, "That's *not* the way it's usually done.")
- that the entire range of services available are explained *before* you start looking at caskets, vaults, etc.
- that all costs were explained, as well as all optional items (Usually, if you are not paying cash, they will want you to use a credit card or sign a formal payment agreement.)
- if they give you their *undivided* attention, without being interrupted by telephone calls, or other staff

3. No one should try to take advantage of your grief.

Arranging a funeral is an ordeal for those who have lost loved ones. It is a business for the funeral director. Therefore, while you might be excused for any breaches of etiquette, he cannot be. He should never try to "shame" you into doing something you don't want to do, or hard sell you any service or product. You should never get the impression that money is more important to them than you are. A good funeral director will make you feel good about your choices.

SUMMARY AND CONCLUSION

Almost without exception, when I've heard of people bemoan the fact they spent more than they could afford on a funeral, it was their own fault. Often, our tendency to overspend is based not so much on sales pressure as it is the pressure of our guilt. We begin to think, If only I had _____! If only I had _____! Then, because it is too late to correct any of the "if onlys," we try to make it up with a lavish funeral.

A good funeral director will not try to persuade you to spend more than you should, but will make you feel comfortable with your selections. That means, should you decide to get the $4,000 package, he won't try to get you to spend $25,000. But if you select the $25,000 package, he won't try to talk you into spending less, either.

Let good taste, reasonableness, and your financial state guide you in planning for a funeral and a funeral service. Don't try to "make up" for any shortcomings in your relationship with the deceased by overspending now. I've seen people buried in far nicer clothes than they could afford when living, and people buy caskets that cost more than the car the deceased drove—*even the house they lived in!*

It's natural to feel guilt when a loved one dies. Few among us ever tell those we love how much we love them. And if we do, we don't say it as often as we should.

Should death intervene before you are able to let your affection be known, don't try to overcome guilt by overspending. Your loved one, your friends, your family, and even your funeral director, if he's the right kind of man, doesn't want you to overspend. God understands all the things you wanted to say and never got around to saying. He will explain.

Funeral directors like to sell "preneed" policies. While evaluating such policies is beyond the scope of this book, I think "preneed" is a good way to handle guilt, especially if you can prearrange without prepaying. That way, all the decisions can be made when you aren't under a cloud of grief and regret.

Speaking of regret, instead of waiting until a loved one is gone and trying to compensate for guilt, get rid of the guilt and let those you love know how much they mean to you. As Bum Phillips once said in a telephone commercial, "Call your momma. I wish I could call mine!" Me, too, Bum. Me, too.

Gymnastics Instructor

OVERVIEW

Gymnastics is an international Olympic sport in which physical exercises are performed in an artistic, yet formally correct, manner. Gymnastics builds self-confidence, fitness, coordination, and good health. While "gym" is taught in public schools, usually their reference is to team sports such as basketball, volleyball, etc. Since you and I have little or no control over any government-run educational programs, we shall look at how to find a professional gymnastics instructor in the private sector.

TIPS AND TACTICS

1. Ask around.

If you've looked up other expert professions in this book, you know that we put a lot of stress on asking friends for recommendations. While their recommendations should never take the place of your "hands-on" inspection, they can help you narrow down your list.

2. Visit the facility.

You should find the staff friendly, open, and cooperative. You should also find:

■ how long they've been in business
■ how much experience their coaches have
■ if their coaches are certified and have attended and/or

are members of such organizations as GAT (Gymnastics Association Training), PDP (Professional Development Program), etc.

- ■ if the coaches have past experience in gymnastics and have participated in competitions
- ■ if the coaches are certified in first aid and CPR
- ■ that everyone is safety conscious, that the coaches talk safety to the students, and that there's proper matting for the sport
- ■ that the coaches treat the children well, and that they encourage as well as correct
- ■ that equipment, shower rooms, lockers, etc., are in good condition

3. Find out about costs.

Just about everyone charges a registration fee. After that, there are differences. Some charge on a graduated scale, with lower fees for younger children. Some charge by the month, while others charge by the session (fall session, winter session, etc.), and still others charge an annual fee. Sometimes you can save money by paying for a longer period, although all things being equal, monthly fees are not only easier to budget, but allow you to cancel without having to negotiate for unused time, or risking financial loss should the facility close.

SUMMARY AND CONCLUSION

When our daughter Rebecca was a child, my wife wanted her to have ballet lessons, not because she thought Rebecca had the potential of becoming the first American ballerina at the Bolshoi Ballet, but because it would give her poise, grace, and a sense of accomplishment. In those days, we didn't know how to go about finding an expert, so she merely enrolled Rebecca in a nearby school. When my wife commented about how dirty the children were after practice, the woman running the school merely snapped, "Well, the janitor only comes in once a week. You can't expect it to remain clean all week." When the bar fell on our child and the instructor was merely irate because the bar would have to be reattached to the wallboard with new molly bolts, Rebecca's career in ballet came to an end. The ballet school itself came to an end shortly thereafter.

How much better off we all would have been had we simply known what to look for and had kept looking! Don't let your aspiring gymnast suffer because you didn't take time to find the right place! There are plenty of good places available, many of which are cleaned daily! With a little patience and persistence, you'll find yours.

Hairstylist

OVERVIEW

When a bald author writes about hairstylists, you know that he is either writing from research or memory. Actually, it's both. Although friends try to console me by saying things such as, "Bald means never having a bad hair day," there is still some to trim around the edges, and, if I don't pay pretty close attention to my hair, I can look like Bozo the clown when I enter and Daddy Warbucks when I exit. The point is, whatever state your hair is in, a good hairstylist can make it look better. (However, the lady who "does" my hair these days still hasn't been able to make me look like Tom Selleck, no matter how extravagantly I tip.)

For those of you who still have your hair, congratulations. I'm not upset with you, as some of my best friends still have their hair. My *wife* still has her hair, and frankly, if one of us had to lose it, I'm glad it was me and not her. However, these tips and tactics will help even those of us who don't have long, beautiful hair like Jane Seymour or King David's favorite son, Absalom.[19]

....

[19] Absalom's hair, incidentally, grew so fast and thick that he weighed five pounds less after a haircut. In fact, his hesitancy to visit his hairstylist at the local tonsorial parlor led to his untimely demise. You can read all about it in II Samuel 14:25; 18:9-14.

For those of you who've recently relocated or are frustrated by your current stylist's failure to make you look like the movie star of your choice, we offer these tips and tactics.

TIPS AND TACTICS

1. Ask someone whose hairstyle you admire,
"Who does your hair?" Admittedly, females will be more comfortable with that question than men. We guys could say, "Hey, Tom, I'm looking for a new barber. Whom do you use?"

2. Look for a hairdresser/hairstylist/beauty operator/ barber who matches your demographic and style profile.
There's an old joke that you should go to the hairstylist with the worst-looking hair because they all trade services, and you can be certain that the one with the awful-looking hair didn't do his or her own! Still, people who style hair for a living know what they like, and if one of them is wearing your hairstyle, they'll understand just what you want. Conversely, you might want to go up to the one with the best-looking hair and ask, "Who did yours?"

This isn't always possible, however, as only women work where I get haircuts and none shave the top of their head to look like me. But I've been in hair emporiums where all the stylists had Muppet hair, and felt certain that none of them would really understand my desire for a conservative cut and style.

3. Look for someone who carries one line of hair-care products.

In my case, that doesn't matter much, because a tube of shampoo will last ten times as long as a tube of toothpaste. But if you're female, or a male with long hair, a hairstylist who carries only one line will *know the line,* and all the products he uses will interact to your advantage.

4. Ask how long it takes to get an appointment.

If they can fit you in the same day, either the hairdresser or the establishment is new, which is not necessarily bad. However, if you can't get an appointment for two weeks, then chances are they won't be able to fit you in when you need them and it's a good idea to look elsewhere.

5. Ask how long they've been in the business.

A recent graduate might not have the experience you want. In Texas, education for a stylist consists of fifteen hundred hours, which pros in the business say, "is only enough time to learn the basics." You want tenure, but you also want someone with the tenacity to continue to study to keep up with the latest trends, techniques, and styles. (If you're still wearing a flattop or a beehive hairdo, you may skip this requirement.)

6. Ask how long it will take to do your hair once you have an appointment.

Again, unless you're me, the correct answer should be thirty to forty-five minutes for women, slightly less for men. Anything less means you're not getting the attention you deserve.

7. Avoid those who juggle customers.

My wife has returned home several times with fried hair as a result of a hairdresser trying to give her a permanent wave while styling someone else's hair. In fact, she just changed hairdressers last week because of that!

8. Avoid those who hard sell.

You are the best judge of what works best for you. Often, a new hairstylist will want to impress you by creating a "whole new look." Usually, this means that the hair length and style you've spent months cultivating will be chopped off in an instant. I remember coming home after my wife had visited such a person and remarking that I thought the Indian wars were over. The long hair I'd encouraged her to grow for years was gone in an instant on the advice of a twenty-year-old woman with orange hair.

9. Watch closely the first time a new person does your hair.

I once went into a new shop and told the hairstylist, "When the fringes around my bald head get this long, the kids say I look like Bozo. Just give me a light trim." The stylist picked up a pair of scissors, and thinking, She can't do too much damage with scissors, I picked up a magazine. When I looked up, I no longer looked like Bozo. I looked like I did the day I got my GI haircut! Worse, my wife, my sister, and all my clients had witty things to say about it. It got so I entered a room warning, "Thank you for not talking about this haircut!"

SUMMARY AND CONCLUSION

I jokingly tell my friends that my life is divided into two great sections: back when I had hair, and now. All the good stories are from the first section. Losing my hair is my biggest regret. My second biggest regret is that I wore a flattop for so long, back when I had hair. My third biggest regret is all the time I spent brushing my hair a hundred strokes each night when I still had some. Considering how much good it did me, I could have employed the time more profitably on other things.

Still, just as an ostrich may admire a bird in flight, I enjoy looking at someone whose hair is nicely done. In our research, our informants tell us that some of the big chains send their hairstylists to their own schools, and that they have a twenty-minute maximum amount of time to spend on each customer, and can be discharged if they continue to exceed that limit. Whether that is true or not, I can't say, as the firm in question declined an opportunity to be interviewed. I'm sure there are great hairdressers and great hair-care establishments of all sizes, from an owner-operated shop with two chairs to the giant chains. However, I wouldn't return to a place where I felt rushed.

Furthermore, I wouldn't return to a place where I was repeatedly kept waiting for my appointment. I remember I once frequented a lady who invariably kept me waiting a half hour. The last appointment I had with her, I found myself waiting *while she did her own hair*! I left, vowing never to return, and have kept that vow for eight years, which makes me suspect I can handle it from here on without problems. Also, as I alluded to earlier, I wouldn't feel comfortable if I went into a place and found that all the stylists had hair colors not found in nature. On the other hand, if that's the kind of look you like, you might feel right at home.

The bottom line on the hairline? Take time to decide what you like, and then find someone you like who can give it to you. Even those among us who are *follically impaired* can find someone who can make us look better.

Hearing Specialist

If you have a hearing problem . . . I said, IF YOU HAVE A HEARING PROBLEM (Sorry, I couldn't resist that!), what do you do? If your hearing loss came suddenly, or if you have drainage, bleeding, or dizziness, you should begin by seeing a physician, especially one who specializes in problems of "eye, ear, nose, and throat." Originally, once a medical doctor had found that there was no treatable physical cause, he either referred you to an audiologist to find out why it had happened or to a hearing specialist to fit you with a hearing aid to amplify sounds in the range where you were having difficulty.

Over the years, some eye, ear, nose, and throat (ENT) specialists began to add audiologists on staff so that they could control not only the fact-finding, but also reap the profit from the hearing aid itself. Then, some audiologists decided that, in addition to testing for physicians, they might as well sell hearing aids, too. So today, you can purchase a hearing aid from an audiologist in your physician's office, from an audiologist operating his or

 her own business, or from a hearing specialist whose primary profession is fitting and selling hearing aids.

If that's not confusing enough, let me add that requirements for audiologists

and hearing specialists vary from state to state. An audiologist has a master's or Ph.D., has undergone a clinical fellowship year, has three hundred supervised clinical hours and has passed a national exam to receive the C.C.C.-A(Certificate of Clinical Competence of Audiology), and is certified by the ASLHA (American Speech-Language and Hearing Association). A hearing specialist, or "hearing-aid specialist," completes a shorter period of study, but is also licensed by the state. Audiologists and hearing specialists use instruments calibrated annually by the state to detect hearing loss. Either professional must refer you to a physician if you advise them that your hearing loss came on suddenly or you have:

- ear pain
- bleeding from the ear
- drainage
- deformation or hole in the ear
- dizziness
- gap of 15db or more between the sound you hear conducted through air and through bone

While there are always exceptions, most hearing-aid specialists give free hearing examinations, and most audiologists charge for that service. Whichever route you travel, follow these tips and tactics!

TIPS AND TACTICS

1. Skip the mail-order ads.
There are many kinds of hearing loss and many ranges of impairment. Don't expect a miracle in the mail. Miracles

don't come cheaply, and one man's miracle is another man's mess. The chances are slim that your particular hearing problem can be solved without someone with the right training and technology determining just what your problem is and selecting a specific solution to solve or, at least, help it.

2. Decide whether you're going to go to an audiologist or a hearing specialist.

■ If an audiologist, make certain he is ASLHA certified, which means he has a master's degree in audiology, has passed the NESPA (National Exam of Speech Pathology and Audiology) with a score of at least six hundred, has been tested by the ASLHA, and is registered with your state board of speech pathology and audiology.

■ If a hearing specialist, make certain that he meets all the requirements of your state, and that his equipment is of current technology and certified by your state.

3. Agree upon reasonable expectations.

If you read some of the ads in magazines, you get the idea that a small piece of plastic and electronics placed in your ear will solve all your hearing problems. Actually, it is only after your audiologist or hearing specialist has examined you and determined the extent and range of your hearing loss that you can learn just how much aid your aid will be. Before you invest in a hearing aid, ask specific questions about what you will and will not be able hear afterward.

4. Know the costs.

Before you agree to purchase any piece of equipment, you have a right to know not only the total cost, but the *operating cost*s for batteries and maintenance. If there is a warranty, it should be spelled out. Does it cover parts *and* labor, or just parts? Do you have to mail it to a repair center, or can repairs be done locally? Is there a guarantee on how quickly repairs will be made?

5. Know that you have a thirty-day trial.

The FDA (Food and Drug Administration) has man-dated that dispensers of hearing aids should allow you a thirty-day period to get accustomed to your equipment and learn what it can and cannot do. If, during that time, you decide you don't want to keep the hearing aid, you may return it. Since the person who sold you the aid will have spent considerable time fitting and counseling, and the returned instrument might or might not be reusable, the FDA *does not* say how much you can be charged for the thirty-day trial period. Some dispensers will take them back and rebate *all* the money you spent on the aid. Others charge one hundred fifty to two hundred dollars. There is a very effective way of finding out, *in advance*, what your provider will charge should the hearing aid not provide the benefit you expect: *you can ask*!

SUMMARY AND CONCLUSION

I have a problem with wax buildup in my ears which I handle with an over-the-counter wax remover and an ear syringe. Upon occasion, my wax problem gets worse before it gets better, as the softened wax flows down against the eardrum. *It is amazing how much harder it is to hear and understand what is going on around me when that happens!* So I feel for those who have a permanent hearing loss! I cannot imagine why someone with such a loss would not rush out and try to correct the cause, or at least alleviate the symptoms with a hearing aid. Yet, many, like my stepmother, just won't. Although she had trouble hearing, she'd say, "No, I'm not ready for *that*!" Here was a lady who wore glasses, dentures, and colored her hair—but somehow, in her mind, wearing a hearing aid was a sign of old age, whereas none of the other was! I tried to no avail to tell her that wearing a hearing aid was no different than wearing glasses, and people of all ages wore them. She merely repeated her opposition, "I'm not ready for *that*!"

If you are not enjoying the sounds of life, love, and laughter around you, your ears are ready for a hearing aid, even if your heart isn't. If you need help, get it. Your friends already know you're hard of hearing anyway!

Hospital Staff

OVERVIEW

There were two giant, well-equipped hospitals in town. Each had its own helicopter; patients whose injuries couldn't wait for an ambulance could be flown in for treatment. Each prided itself on its cardiac-care facilities. In every way, they competed for patients, honors, and services. Yet, once you were inside as a patient or a visitor, there was a world of difference.

In Hospital A, personnel passed you in the halls without so much as a passing glance. In Hospital B, medical personnel smiled and said, "Hello," and if you seemed lost, they asked if they could direct you somewhere for help. Back in Hospital A, the staff obviously brooked no nonsense from family or patients. Family was tolerated, and patients were cared for with machinelike precision but with an air that the nursing staff had better things to do. In Hospital B, medicine was practiced at a personal level and the nursing staff looked at the patients, talked with them, and listened to them. Which hospital would *you* rather be in?

Is your choice of a hospital important? While it *could* mean the difference between life and

death, it is much more likely to mean the difference between health and prolonged sickness. Statistics indicate that *20 percent* of the patients who go into a hospital leave it with an infection they didn't have when they arrived. The right hospital can also make a difference in your financial health because some hospitals are more prone to billing errors than others.

Therefore, you want a hospital that not only takes care of your medical problem but goes all out to see that they don't create one while you're there. You want one that watches out for your financial health, too. That requires a good, caring staff, from administration, to nursing, to nurses aides. Here's how to find one!

TIPS AND TACTICS

1. Ask your physician what hospital he's affiliated with. If you have a good doctor, he will practice at a good hospital or, preferably, *hospitals.* A study in Washington, D.C., and San Francisco revealed that 50 percent of physicians use a single hospital for 95 percent of their cases, 30 percent use two hospitals, and less than 10 percent use four or more hospitals. I would feel more comfortable with a physician who used more than one facility, so he could match each hospital's specialty to my need. (If you don't have a good doctor, read the section under "How to Find an Expert: Doctor.") Call the state board of hospitals and see if there are any complaints against the hospital(s) he mentioned.

2. Call the hospital and ask for the administrative department.

Explain that you are looking for a hospital in the area and realize that, just as with any medical facility, some are better than others. Ask:

- Is yours a teaching hospital? Teaching hospitals usually have experts supervising everything. However, since they are teaching, some of your care might be provided by student interns, although in most cases student nurses are always accompanied by an RN.

- What procedures is the hospital equipped to handle? If your problem requires a high degree of specialization, you'll want a hospital that specializes in that procedure. If yours is a low-risk case, you will want a hospital that is clean, close, efficient, and courteous.

- Do you provide itemized bills? They must if you ask for one, but it would be nice if they offered the service as a matter of course. Whenever you are released from any hospital, you should check to make certain that any canceled tests weren't billed, that you actually received all the medication you were billed for, and that any tests that were redone because of staff error were not rebilled. Since some patients might not have been well enough to know what procedures were performed, it is good to check with family members. Since most hospitals will provide a "sleeping chair" for family members of seriously ill patients, it's a good idea to have that family member jot down what was done, by whom, and when.

■ Is your hospital JCAHO (Joint Counsel for the Accreditation of Healthcare Organizations) approved? Membership in this organization is not required, but many of the better hospitals pay JCAHO to come in and survey their services and facilities to see if they're up to standards.

3. Visit the hospital.

Ask the administrative department for an outpatient service list and a directory of physicians that practice in that hospital. Tell them you'd like to find the right hospital on a preneed basis and would like a tour. For openers, you'll want to tour the emergency room and see how it's equipped. (This is especially important if you have children!) If there might be a baby in your future, ask to tour the OB section. See how the waiting rooms and the ICU waiting rooms are equipped, and how the family and friends are treated.

4. Visit friends who are in that hospital.

That profound philosopher Yogi Berra once said, "You can observe a lot just by watching." Are patients treated as individuals or case numbers? If the patient is not seriously ill, a nurse should observe him every few *hours*. Seriously ill patients should be observed every few *minutes*. Nurses should answer calls at once. They should spend time with patients to ask about any changes in condition, any pain, and any new complaints. They should call the doctor if an unexpected change occurs. In short, they should treat you as if you were what you are: a *customer*, without whom they would not have jobs.

SUMMARY AND CONCLUSION

Your chances of "needing" surgery depend on where you live, because doctors in some communities are much more aggressive when it comes to surgery than are doctors in neighboring communities. These facts came to light not as a result of research done by some antimedical group, but by a study done by Dartmouth Medical School. Dartmouth found, for instance, that 75 percent of elderly men in one Maine town had undergone prostate surgery. In an adjacent town of the same size, less than 25 percent had undergone the procedure. Coincidence or greedy physicians? The issue is debatable. Most physicians, however, will admit that we perform much more surgery than is required in this country. English surgeons perform about half as many surgeries as do American surgeons, yet the mortality rate is about the same. According to the Rand Corporation, 40 percent of all heart bypasses produce no patient merit. Other studies show that well over 30 percent of those who have bypasses suffer some degree of brain damage due to their hours spent on the heart-lung machine. Other studies show that at least a third of all hysterectomies performed were unnecessary.[20]

If surgery is required, of course, you want to have it done by the best surgeon in the best hospital. However, we need to be aware that major surgery can not only

....

[20] Nor do all physicians advise patients that the damage done to nerves in the operation might affect their sex lives afterward.

create major health problems, but major financial problems. A forty-state audit of hospital bills exceeding ten thousand dollars showed errors in 93 percent of them. The most common overcharges were for treatments never given, followed by lab tests never performed and medicines never given.[21]

Your hospital exists to meet the needs of the patients whose doctors practice there. Therefore, it is very, very important that, before you have a need for medical care, you find not only the right hospital, but the right physician. If you find the right hospital first, then it makes sense to begin your search for the right physician by asking the hospital for a list of physicians who practice there.

A good, caring physician and a good, caring hospital operate under the Hippocratic oath, remembering to "do thy patient no harm." They will work with you to see that you get the level of care you need without unnecessary tests, unnecessary treatments, or unnecessary surgeries. It has to do with ethics, with principles, with care. You can find it—if you try.

[21] From *The Secrets of the Atkins Center,* by Dr. Robert C. Atkins, Wellness Communications, Inc.

Income Tax Preparer

OVERVIEW

The thirteen American colonies became the United States of America as a protest against high taxes—specifically, taxation without representation. If our founding fathers had known how high taxes would become *with representation*, they might well have paid the tea tax and toasted King George with their favorite beverage, for taxes in colonial times weren't a tithe on a tithe of taxes today.

Today, we pay a tax on every dollar we earn to the federal government and, in all but four states, the state government as well. In addition, many cities collect income tax, and in some places, if you live in one city and work in another, or live in one state and work in another, you have to pay income taxes to "all of the above." In addition to straight income tax, so-called Social Security taxes, also tagged to income, take an additional 15.3 percent.[22] In addition to taxes on our income, our homes, businesses, and real estate are taxed on their value by city, county, school, and even hospital districts and/or road and bridge

---

[22] Some would say the actual number is half that, as the employee pays half, and the employer *has* to pay the other half. However, an employer looks at the *total cost* of an employee. Consequently, the money ultimately comes out of the employee's pocket.

districts. If we have anything left and try to spend it, it is exposed to one final tax, the sales tax, on its way out of our hands. If we try to hang on to it for a rainy day, any interest the money accrues, even if it doesn't keep pace with inflation, gets taxed, too. (Perhaps none of this would have happened if your forefathers had protested taxes by tossing the collectors into the sea instead of just the tea!)

Ironically, income taxes didn't come along until Lincoln needed money to fight the Civil War. After the war, tax protesters took the matter of income tax to the Supreme Count, which ruled it unconstitutional and repealed the income tax law! (No, no one got their illegally garnered tax dollars back. Don't you know government better than that?) Of course, government, having found a new source of income, regardless of how briefly or illegally, was hooked and, like any junkie, wanted not only to maintain the current dosage, but increase it. They weren't able to put into effect an income tax law by the Supreme Court again, however, until 1913. At the time, those opposed to the measure said, "Income tax will be a creeping thing that will stifle initiative." Those in favor retorted, "That's ridiculous! The American people would never pay more than 10 percent: they'd riot in the streets!"

If you've gone back and totaled your percentage of taxes and wondered why you aren't rioting in the streets, it's because of a little trick Congress came out with in 1943 called "pay-as-you-go." Prior to that, taxpayers had to pay their taxes once a year, which made them very, very aware of every penny. However, with income tax withholding, people never saw the money that went for taxes, so they didn't really realize it was gone. It's similar to the old biology experiment of placing a frog in a pan of warm water and gradually raising the temperature. If the rise is gradual enough, the frog never gets suspicious, and will sit there and boil without trying to escape.

Because our tax rise has taken place slowly, over time, and oft consisted of "temporary taxes" that became permanent,[23] we have allowed ourselves to be boiled without protest. Consequently, according to an encyclopedia at my elbow, "European nations, with exceptions, impose lighter income taxes than the United States. . . .The U.S. yield at all levels of government is 16 percent of total tax revenues, the European only 7 percent."[24] Admittedly, my encyclopedia is a few years out of date, but the trend in recent years has been for *more* and *higher* taxes, not fewer and lower. (In my own state, every time OPEC drops the price of oil a few cents, the state raises the gasoline tax a corresponding amount, figuring if we never get the benefit of the lower price, we won't notice that we received a tax hike.) Meanwhile, tax laws have become increasingly complex to the extent that a recent IRS head admitted to Congress that *he* didn't fully

[23] The "temporary" tax placed on telephone service for the duration of the Korean War is a good example. The telephone company fought for three decades after the war ended to have it removed, succeeded for a couple of months in the 1980s, only to see it reinstituted. After divestiture, it was retitled an "end-user charge."

[24] *Encyclopedia International,* Lexicon Publications, volume 17, page 520.

understand all of them! As bad as our taxes are today, in the future, we will look back on these as the "good old days of light taxation." A recent report by the GAO (Government Accounting Office) said that, by 2012, funding for "entitlements" alone would *exceed* current projected tax revenues.

Daniel Webster, an American statesman who died in 1852, long before income taxes came about and other taxes got out of hand, said, "Now is the time that men work quietly in the fields, and women weep softly in the kitchen; the legislature is in session, and no man's property is safe." His point was well taken, for every time the legislature meets, a larger share of our property is transferred to the state.

Now that I've gotten that off my chest, let me advise that you can't get out of paying your taxes (ask Leona Helmsley). But you can make certain that you don't pay a penny more than you should if you get the right tax advice. Here are some tips to help you do just that.

TIPS AND TACTICS

1. Turn to the front of the book and read the section on "accountant."

If your tax situation is quite complex, you might be better off with a CPA. On the other hand, if it is of average difficulty and everything can be handled on a standard 1040, you'll pay less to have it done by a tax preparer. (If your tax situation fits the criteria for the short form, you can do your taxes yourself and save even more.)

2. Ask around.

If you'd like a list of good, qualified tax preparers, call your banker or the National Association of Accountants, who will give you the names of qualified people in your area. You can also ask friends, but as you do, remember that different people judge tax preparers by different standards. For instance, three people I know are each ecstatic about a different tax preparer for three different reasons!

■ One says, "Mine charges me practically nothing!"

■ One says, "I get a big tax refund each year!"

■ One says, "Mine charges quite a bit, but he must be good because he's been doing my taxes for ten years and neither of us ever spent a night in jail."

It is possible, of course, that the one that charges practically nothing is really doing a good job, but is a quick, inexpensive job getting you all the tax breaks you deserve? It is also possible that you overlooked something that your tax preparer found, resulting in a big refund. However, a big refund *every year* means that you've been paying too much in taxes and that your money has been lying around in a government warehouse without drawing any interest. (If you have money you want stored at no interest, send it to me!) And while no tax preparer or payer wants to go to jail, we certainly want every *legal* deduction we can take! Best bet: Get names from your friends and then check them through other sources.

3. Decide what size firm you want.

There are several large, national chains that offer tax

preparation assistance. In addition, there are numerous smaller, individual firms. Each has advantages and disadvantages.

■ Large firms will have formal training programs, supervisors, and frequently, on-line tax help with the home office. On the other hand, because they charge much less than CPAs and are somewhat less expensive than independents, their profit depends on throughput; that is, processing as many returns per hour as possible. This means they cannot always take time to ferret out all deductions you are entitled to take. Also, large firms tend to hire extra help during tax season, and these preparers might not be as experienced as their regular staff. So should you or the IRS have a question later, the person who did your taxes might not be around to provide an answer.

■ Small firms offer continuity. They'll be there to help you if the IRS has a question and to answer a tax question during the year. They can usually spend a bit more time doing your return and will give you valuable advice to negate problems or pick up deductions on your next return. The downside is that they might not have the backup tax professionals on call like a large firm. While they can always call the IRS to clarify a point, the IRS lines are usually backed up around tax time.

4. Be wary of come-ons.

Ads that say, "instant tax refund" *usually* mean that they'll *lend* you the money they compute you have coming back from the government for a fee. It's usually a high-interest loan that you'll owe regardless of whether or not the tax refund actually materializes.

SUMMARY AND CONCLUSION

Elvis Presley was so afraid of an IRS audit that he let them do his taxes, figuring that way there would be no gray areas. Having the IRS do your taxes does not guarantee that you'll get every legal deduction or that your tax return will be done correctly. What, the IRS could make mistakes? Right. When I was with Scripps-Howard newspapers, each year we would send the same tax data to a half-dozen different IRS offices and print the results—which were always totally different. Besides, even if the errors were made by the IRS, you will be held accountable.

The Internal Revenue Service is composed of overworked agents who are there to answer your tax questions as clearly and concisely as possible. When the laws are so complex that the head honcho doesn't understand them, you can't expect more from the regular troops. However, they are really nice people, and they're not there to try and put you in jail for an honest mistake, they're just there to enforce compliance.[25] And if you're in a bind, they'll work with you to set up a payment schedule. I know. Been there. Done that.

....

[25] Tax laws are written by our beloved Congress in an ongoing attempt to distribute your earnings in enough different places that they can be reelected to do it to you again. (Karl Marx said that democracy would endure until the citizens learned they could vote themselves money.) I like the way a wag put it better: Any government that robs Peter to pay Paul is certain to have the support of Paul!

Insurance Agent

OVERVIEW

Insurance is a device for pooling risks, and goes back as far as recorded civilization. Six thousand years ago, the residents of the Tigris and Euphrates valleys had insurance policies. Hammurabi, king of Babylon around 1800 B.C., wrote a code of laws regarding insuring overland shipments against loss. From Babylon, the concept of insurance spread to the seafaring people of Phoenicia, where underwriters began insuring ships and cargoes. By the time Rome became a world power, both "term" and "whole life" insurance policies were being sold. By the third century, Ulpian constructed a table of life annuity values by age that was used until it was replaced by more accurate tables in the 1800s.

Lloyd's of London, one of the most famous insurers of all time, began as a coffeehouse on the Thames in the late 1600s where individual patrons would agree to pledge a certain amount of money against the safe arrival of ships and cargoes. In case of loss, no company, but *the participating patrons,* were liable for the loss.

Today, insurance is one of the largest industries in the world. Virtually anything can be insured against loss or damage. Even satellites are insured against loss during launch or premature "death" in space. Whatever your personal insurance needs, here's how you find the right agent!

TIPS AND TACTICS

1. Decide what kind of agent you want.
There are two basic types of insurance agents: "captive" and "independent." A "captive" agent represents a single insurance company. An "independent" agent usually represents several companies. The benefit of a "captive" agent is that he is usually well trained by the company and has a thorough knowledge of all its products. The benefit of an "independent" agent is that he can pick and choose among companies to get you the best coverage at the best price.

If you choose to go with a "captive" agent, you'll need to get one whose company can offer coverage to meet all of your insurance needs, or you will need to deal with more than one agent. If you choose to go with an "independent" agent, you'll need to make certain that all of the companies you deal with are A.M. Best-rated "A."

2. Look for a well-trained agent.
There are national accreditation programs for insurance agents. If you're looking for life insurance, look for an agent with an LUTC (Life Underwriting Training) or CLU (Certified Life Underwriter) after his name. The professional credential that relates to property and casualty insurance is CPCU (Chartered Property and Casualty Underwriter.) He will have *proven* his knowledge of the business. Also, since laws and products change continually, agents who have exhibited the talent and

tenacity to attain these certifications are more likely to make the effort to keep up with the most current data.

3. Look for a company you can trust.

There are many good insurance companies that don't advertise or that advertise very little. Ask your prospective insurance agent if the company under consideration is A.M. Best-rated and, if so, what that rating is. You want a company rated A or better. (A Best rating does not rate companies by how they pay claims, but on the basis of stability, assets, and reserves.) If you're considering health insurance, call a few hospitals, ask for the insurance claims section, and *ask how well that company pays!* In addition, most states have an insurance commission. Call 1-800-555-1212 to find out the number of the insurance commission's consumer division. Then ask the commission if the company under consideration has an inordinate number of problems.

4. Look for an agent you can trust.

A really good insurance agent will be more interested in long-term *service* than short-term *sales*. True, he will make his living through sales, but his demeanor, attitude, and presentation will be geared toward finding out what your goals and needs are and finding ways to help you meet those needs. A good agent will:

- present himself in a professional manner
- suggest ways to serve you, not just try to sell you
- be committed to the industry, not just "selling insurance" until he finds a job he likes better (Tenure is important in any profession.)

be able to answer your questions clearly and concisely

be willing to admit when he doesn't know, and be willing to find the answers to your questions

be willing to help you decide what you want, not wanting to talk you into what he wants you to have

be able to answer questions about the time in business, history, track record, payment policy, etc., about any company he represents

ask logical questions about your goals and ambitions

A good agent will *not*:

handle any company that isn't A.M. Best-rated "A" or better (Best ratings are as follows: A+ excellent, A+, A, A-, B+, B, etc. Best does not assign failing grades, but most companies that expect a poor rating won't apply for a rating at all.)

play on your emotions, painting pictures of starving spouses and children, your death of a curable disease languishing outside a hospital, etc. (In spite of the rhetoric, it is possible for the persistent to get indigent health care. We even provide it for *illegal* immigrants!)

start talking insurance as an investment (unless discussing annuity)

suggest or agree to falsifying an application for insurance (Not only is this a violation of the law, but also if discovered, your insurance will be revoked and you will not have been covered for any claim!)

offer to give you part of your money back from his commission

- promise guaranteed coverage while your application is still pending approval at the home office

5. *Look out for yourself.*

It's a sad thing to outlive your insurance company, or to find that your health was better than theirs! This won't happen if you pick a well-rated company or if you live in a state such as Texas, which has an insurance pool requiring other companies authorized to do business within the state to cover the policyholders of any company that goes belly up. You can also help yourself by:

- being cautious whenever anyone suggests that you replace one policy with another
- making certain that your agent has an "errors and omissions" policy (That covers you in case he screws up your policy.)
- never buying a policy on the day it's explained to you (Always take the material, study it carefully, and comparison shop before making your decision.)
- never buying from an agent who won't leave you a copy of the material he is showing you
- never buying from anyone who uses scare or pressure tactics

SUMMARY AND CONCLUSION

I have always believed that it had to be difficult to sell that first life insurance policy. "Ugh," says the representative from the Paleolithic Insurance Company, as he comes up to a cave dweller. He then says, "Dork, here's the deal. You give us ten clams a month as long as you live, and when you die, we'll give the person of your choice *ten thousand clams*!" You can almost see old Dork roll his eyes and exclaim, "I give you *what*?"

On the surface, that first life insurance policy must have been a hard sell. You pay on something as long as you live and when you're dead, you collect. Yet, for thousands of years, people have been taking money they could have spent on themselves and giving it to insurance companies to take care of those that will survive them. I think that says a lot about the basic goodness of our character. When you think about it, health insurance, car insurance, and home insurance, are all ways of saying, "I'm responsible. I care." Corporations who insure executives, aircraft, ships, and satellites are saying the same thing to their shareholders and employees. "We're responsible. We care. We want things to continue even in the event of loss."

Buying insurance is not only a matter of showing your loved ones that you care, but many insurance policies (such as auto liability) are required by law. Follow the tips and tactics in this section, and you'll find what you need and an agent who is on your side whenever a need arises.

Interior Designer/ Decorator

My wife reads the decorator magazines, and they are certainly a good place to start when you're beginning to wonder if the gifts you brought back from Graceland and the stuffed armadillo you won at the raffle really look all that good with your Queen Anne furniture. Some of the decorator magazines are, to my taste, a bit far out. I've seen photos of furniture and even curtain rods made out of tree limbs with the bark still on them. Another showed a decorator's home who was into Zen. Her home was all in white, with bare wood floors. No wall hangings. No photos. No electronics. No furniture, save a small white table and a single chair in a bare kitchen. She slept on a pallet, took a makeup kit to the bathroom, and returned everything to a closet when she finished so the apartment would look unoccupied, as though her passing had no effect on her environment.

Hey, if you like living in the sticks or living in an empty pad, that's fine—I'm sure there are decorators who can catch the vision and help you. For me, I tend to go with comfortable furniture and wouldn't own a coffee table I couldn't *carefully* use as a footstool. Yet, difference of opinion is what makes for interesting horse races—and decorators.

Despite my earlier crack about Graceland, I haven't been there, but I remember what one visitor said: "It destroys the myth that taste comes with money." In fact, in one of my wife's decorator magazines (Okay, I read them *occasionally!*), a decorator said, "Every night I pray that people with money will get taste and that people with taste will get money."

Frankly, whether you have money with no taste or taste with no money, the right decorator can help you do great things to your home or apartment. Here's how to go about finding one.

TIPS AND TACTICS

1. Talk to friends.
Particularly talk to friends who have similar tastes. Ask them if they had help with decorating or design, and, if so, ask for the name of the person they worked with.

2. Interview several decorators or designers in person.
Tell them you're considering redecorating and:

■ Tell them your budget. Before you waste any of your (or their) time, let them know what you can spend and whether or not you are flexible. If they are still willing to talk with you, proceed as follows.

■ Ask about their credentials. There are degrees in interior design. Some designers are registered, and some states require testing before licensing. Depending on what you are wanting to do, this might or might not be important to you. Find out how long they've been in the business, what local and national organizations they belong to, etc. Usually, someone at a local furniture store will help you match sofa and tables to lamps. If carpet and drapes are all you want, you probably don't need someone from the ASID (American Society of Interior Designers). However, as with any other purchase, as the stakes get higher, you'll want a higher level of expertise.

- Ask to look at their portfolios.
- Ask what they like to do. While most designers are flexible, if yours is an avant-garde-type person and you're firmly committed to Queen Anne, you might have problems.
- Allow yourself to be questioned. The designer should probe to get an idea of what you want. Are you thinking just of furniture? Carpet and drapes? Architectural? What styles do you like? What colors? Do you want him to be responsible for all or part of it?
- Determine if he is dedicated to getting you the look you want, or simply wants to get you to go with the look he wants you to have. Never work with anyone who is pushy, rude, or who doesn't take your thoughts and feelings into consideration.
- Get references. References, of course, are of no value unless you take the time to check them.
- Find out all the costs—in writing. A usual fee for consultation can range from fifty to one hundred fifty dollars

and should include an itemized list and prices. This covers only the plan. If you want the designer to be involved in locating the proper pieces, seeing that everything is done properly, etc., that will require more of his time and your money. Never pay for the entire cost up front, even if you're promised a discount. (Go back and read "How to Find an Expert: Building Contractor.")

SUMMARY AND CONCLUSION

It was legendary architect Frank Lloyd Wright who said, "Doctors can bury their mistakes. All an architect can do is suggest that you plant vines." Since vines don't grow all that well indoors, before you rush out, hire a decorator, and do something drastic, take time to stop and think about it. After all, when you redecorate, whether it's a room or an entire home, you're probably going to have to live with it for a long while. Will these changes stand the test of time? Will they enhance or hamper your lifestyle? Is the "new look" something that will bring you years of pleasure or years of frustration? Davy Crockett, whose idea of decorating was to make sure that the logs were all chinked with mud and the dirt floor was packed tight, nevertheless gave some advice that will help when you're decorating: "Be *sure* you're right; then go ahead."

Janitor/Maid

OVERVIEW

The term *janitor* dates back to the sixteenth century and comes from *janus*, which is Latin for "arch or gate." Janitors were originally keepers of the gate, keeping the premises clean. Today, the word *janitor* is often used as a synonym for *maid*, which comes from the middle English *maide*, which originally meant maiden, but now means, according to the dictionary, a woman employed to do domestic work. If that's not muddled enough, today some *maids* are men.

Whether you call them *janitors, maids,* or *domestic help*, you call them when you have neither the time nor the inclination to keep your home or office clean yourself. Here's how to find the right dust buster for you!

TIPS AND TACTICS

1. Ask friends.

Friends are a great source of references because they can tell you if a janitor's *performance* matches the *promise*. Questions you'll want to ask include:

■ What will he clean?
■ What will he *not* clean?
■ Is he reliable? (If it's a service instead of an individual,

will they send someone else if your regular person
should be unavailable?)

Have you ever had cause to question his honesty?

Have things been broken or damaged? If so, did he tell
you, or did you discover it later?

What does he charge? What is included in that charge?

What is specifically not included or is an extra?

**2. *Call in response to ads in the newspaper and/or Yel-
low Pages.***

Ask these questions:

What experience do you have?

Can you furnish references? (Remember, references
are of no value unless you check them!)

What do you charge?

What is included in that charge?

What is not included in the charge? What does it cost
to do those items?

Are you (or your firm) reliable? (If it's a service instead
of an individual, ask, "Will you send someone else if
my regular person should be unavailable?)

Are you (or your company) bonded and insured?

Do you have several clients? (Under current tax law, if
the person has several clients and is an independent
contractor, you do not have to withhold taxes, social
security, and other government taxes. If they do not,
you must if your payment exceeds an ever-decreasing
minimum.[26])

....

[26] You must check the tax laws at the time of employment, as when the Legislature is in
session, they show how wise we were to elect them by continually issuing laws, rules,
and regulations; all of which require additional tax money to enforce.

3. Interview the leading contender(s) in person.

If the leading contender(s) is a company, visit their offices, ask for brochures, and ask to see a copy of their insurance, etc. If the leading contender(s) is an individual, you can expect him to come to your home or office. During this interview, be very specific about what will and will not be done. For instance, if the normal service includes dusting and polishing, bathroom cleaning, kitchen cleaning, sweeping, scrubbing, and vacuuming carpets, but doesn't include windows, ovens, grills, refrigerator, chandeliers, or baseboards, determine how often such should be cleaned and what the fee is. Also, it is a good idea to keep a printed list of what is agreed to and when it is to be done in case a service sends you someone new or your individual forgets.

SUMMARY AND CONCLUSION

Time was when Father worked to support Mother and the children, and Mother stayed home, took care of the house, the children, and Father. Whether you feel those were the "good old days" or the "bad old days," they are, nevertheless, the *old days*. Today, Mother and Father usually have jobs outside the home. That means that the hand that rocks the cradle and the hand that cleans the house is often that of a professional worker from outside the family. Most who use maid or janitorial services do not use their services every day. Yet, it is nice to have someone reliable to depend upon to do the chores we don't have time or the inclination to do ourselves.

If you use the tips and tactics outlined, you should have no trouble finding the person (or service) right for you. But, remember that needs, organizations, and people change. If you find, after a while, that it isn't working out, don't be afraid to say, "Hey, this isn't working out. I think it'd be better if I found someone else." It's not like you were firing Mom, for goodness sake, so do what is right for you!

We have had some interesting domestic help over the years, and some have since achieved legendary status. There was the one lady who, alone and unaided, routinely flipped the king-size mattress. She was a real whiz of a worker, but had to be discharged because she kept getting into the gin . . . but never used a glass. Then, there was the one who took home toilet paper, bar soap, and of all things, baking powder! One wanted to just sit and talk and be our best friend at her usual hourly rate. Another cleaned like she thought she was a cross between Mary Poppins and Samantha of *Bewitched,* only her magic dusting wand, dabbed here and there, didn't really solve the problem. Another cleaned with a passion, even taking down paintings and pictures, and cleaning the backs, except she never could tell when they were level afterward, not even when I bought her a level. Another always had a specific, somewhat scary, "word from the Lord" for us. Another always wanted to get an advance on her salary, but then wouldn't come in at all until she was desperate. And, along the way, some were warm, helpful, did what they were asked, and went away with minimal disruption to our lives. Following the tips and tactics above will help you get the latter kind of maid, janitor, or domestic worker.

Jeweler

OVERVIEW

There is no national standard one must meet to call one-self a "jeweler." In that regard, it's sort of like being a writer. You get an office, some merchandise, hang a sign, print business cards, stationery, and there you are. Since anyone can open a store and use the term, the old Latin phrase, *cravat emptor*, "let the buyer beware," applies. I had a very valuable nugget gold ring ruined when I went to a jeweler who said he could "stretch" it half a size. In-stead, he broke it, charged fifty-five dollars to repair it, and to my surprise, the repair was smooth gold! I later found that many community colleges teach a six-week "jeweler" course. Six weeks' training doesn't sound like much,[27] and it isn't, but one need not even attend *that* to call oneself a "jeweler." There is much truth in the old Persian proverb, "The *buyer* needs a thousand eyes, the *seller*, none."

Here are some tips to finding a jeweler who won't rip you off or ruin your heirlooms!

TIPS AND TACTICS

1. Get recommendations.
Ask your friends who they would recommend, realizing

[27] By way of comparison, my home state requires fifteen hundred hours of instruction to cut hair.

that they can be (and might have been) fooled, too! Also, ask the Better Business Bureau if it has had any complaints.

2. Case the joint.

Go in and look around. As Yogi Berra said, "You can *observe* a lot *just by watching.*" Do you feel comfortable in the surroundings? Do you feel comfortable with the person who is waiting on you? Do you feel pressured and looked down upon, or do you feel welcome, as if serving you is a pleasure?

3. Tenure counts.

Ask how long they've been in business and if they're planning to stay in business in that location.

4. Ask for credentials.

If one piece of jewelry is significantly more than a similar-looking piece, ask them to explain why. Ask what experience the jeweler has had in appraising stones. Ask if he is qualified to give an *insurance appraisal,* and *if so,* what percentage of the value of the piece could be covered by insurance.

5. Talk to the one who'll do the work.

If you are leaving a piece to be repaired or having something specially designed, *insist on speaking to the one who will do the work.* Ask what experience he has. Ask to see some examples of his work and for the names of some customers he's worked for that you can call. If you do this in a nice, nonthreatening way, there is no reason he should be upset by this. Even honored ambassadors have to present their credentials to heads of state.

6. Ask if they're insured for theft.

You have every right to feel uneasy leaving a valuable piece of jewelry (or a treasured heirloom) with a jeweler who isn't properly insured.

7. Ask about appraisals.

Most people like to have a *retail* appraisal, but all that does is double your insurance premiums because the insurance company is going to replace your loss at a cost near wholesale anyway! (Beware of any jewelers who give you an appraisal without first cleaning the piece.)

8. Be wary of "quick-set" jewelry repair.

You frequently find places in malls that will repair jewelry while you wait. To be certain the repair will hold, jewelry must first be cleaned ultrasonically or in boiling water. If you're dealing with quality jewelry, it's important that the person doing the cleaning knows what he is doing. While diamonds are our hardest substance, they can get a smoky appearance if improperly cleaned, and acids can actually burn dirt into a piece of jewelry.

SUMMARY AND CONCLUSION

If you want to purchase an "off the shelf" made-in-Japan wristwatch, you're probably as well off in a discount store. But, if you want a quality piece of jewelry *and don't know jewelry, then you'd better get to know your jeweler!* This is one area where taking the time to get all your questions answered is time well spent. Just because one place sells a half-carat diamond ring in a fourteen-karat gold setting for half as much as another, it does not necessarily follow that the first place has a real bargain. The second place might be charging less for what you get, because the biggest difference in price is not the *size of the stone but the quality*. For instance, in diamonds, the value is based on *cut, clarity*, and *carat* weight. Also, today there are many high-quality, low-cost, synthetic stones on the market. Certain unscrupulous jewelers have been known to sell these as genuine, or, as one popular investigative TV program revealed recently, *replace the stones in your existing jewelry with fakes!*

Best advice: Know your jeweler.

Landscaper

OVERVIEW

If you want to have your lawn cared for, read the section under "How to Find an Expert: Lawn-Care Professional." If you want to have a lawn *worth* caring for, then, you've come to the right place.

Our first two homes were both in subdivisions developed by a single builder. In the first instance, several hundred home owners lived in one of just eight different models. If, for example, you lived in the Hiltonian model, you had the same front elevation (appearance) as all the other Hiltonians, the same floor plan, the same walls, the same wallpaper, the same carpet, tile, stove, sink, etc., etc., ad nauseam. When we bought our second home, the elevations were all different, but there were only about three floor plans. When a neighbor invited you for dinner, you knew where the bathroom was, the closet, the sink, the circuit breaker, etc., because it was the same place as yours.

Even the plants were identical. Same Japanese boxwood hedges, even the same trees: two fruitless mulberries in the front lawn, one in the back. All made out of ticky-tacky. All looking just the same.

Many builders served the area where we bought our third home, so it was unique. However, the lot was much the way it had been when God had finished with the area. Of course, back when God had it, it didn't matter if the shallow ditch in the back ran like Niagara during those heavy East Texas spring rains! After the house and lawn were in, however, those heavy rains tended to take out the flower beds!

What did we do? We called a professional landscaper so we could bring not just *beauty* to our lawn, but beauty that could survive when it rained like Genesis.

Is your lawn just like your neighbor's? Or is it merely uneven or even uninteresting? If so, here's what you do to make it as unique and special as you are!

TIPS AND TACTICS

1. Ask around.

Ask the neighbor whose lawn you envy who landscaped his place. Or drive out and just look at homes you like, ring the doorbell, and pop the question. You're thinking you can't do it, but you can. Just ding-dong, and say, "Hello, I'm _____, and I couldn't help noticing what a beautiful job you've done landscaping. Would you mind telling me who you used?" Or drive by a new area under development and see who is putting in lawns you admire.

If you're too shy for these tactics, check "landscaping" in the Yellow Pages. However, whenever you check the Yellow Pages, remember that the firm with the biggest ad might not be the best qualified or most experienced. Many well-established firms rely more on word of mouth than advertising, and someone has to pay for those large, expensive, display ads.

2. Make certain they know what they're doing.

In some states, landscapers are licensed. You can tell by checking all the ads in the telephone book. If one list says "licensed" or lists a license number, you can at least know that licensing is an option. Those with smaller ads might not list their license number, so you'll have to ask if they're licensed and take their license number to make certain. Many states also have landscape organizations which share information and uphold the high standards of the industry. In Texas, for example, there's TALC (Texas Association of Landscape Contractors). Licensing and membership in a professional organization is a definite plus, because it shows commitment.

3. Call the leading contenders.

During this call, you ask:

- Does our state license landscapers?
- If so, is your firm licensed?
- How long has your firm been in business? (Five or more years is good.)
- What is your educational background? (A degree in horticulture, or a landscape architecture would be good.)
- Do you carry liability insurance? (This is important not only in case they damage your property moving in trees, etc., but in case some of their employees get hurt on your property. Otherwise, injured employees could sue you! No, life isn't always fair.)

■ Do you give free estimates? (Most will measure your lawn, check your soil, and give you a written estimate that includes what plants they will use free. Others will even provide a sketch showing where the plants will go and what changes they will make.)

4. Have at least two come out to your home.

They should talk with you to determine what you like and don't like, as well as your budget. They should then provide you with *at least* a complete written description of what they will do and where and, at best, a sketch. Really good ones will give you options; one option that gives you a good landscape design within your budget and another option that gives you a *great* landscape design for slightly more. In addition they should:

■ offer to provide you with detailed care instructions for all the plants they provide

■ provide a guarantee of six months to a year on plants, trees, and grass (They would, naturally, include a proviso that you would have to water and care for the plants according to instructions.)

SUMMARY AND CONCLUSION

Time, the Bible says, began in a garden, and God Himself was the master landscaper. Even after all the years of human mismanagement, even the most callous'd' among us would have to admit that He does good work. Still, by the time the building contractors have left the area, most lawns could use some work. Few among us have the skill and knowledge to look at a parcel of land, think up the right arrangement of plants, the right de-sign, and then make it happen. Choosing the right land-scaper can make your home more beautiful and enjoyable for the rest of your life or the life of the mort-gage. (And if you move, it'll make your home much, much more salable.)

Lawn-Care Professional

OVERVIEW

I love a beautiful lawn, yet I hate, loathe, and despise yard work.[28] If we lived on an eighty-by-one-hundred-foot lot, that would be no problem, but we live on two and one-half acres in an area of nice homes on similarly sized lots. Therefore, a beautiful lawn is not only the neighborhood standard, but difficult to obtain and maintain.

Years ago, when we lived on an acre lot, as I was putting the lawn mower away, a thought came into my head: Only God knows how much I hate yard work. Therefore, I went in and told my wife, "There must be someone in a country of this size that doesn't hate yard work as much as I do and doesn't make as much money. Therefore, all I have to do is find that person and my troubles are over."

---

[28] Until 1928, the White House lawn was mowed by a small flock of sheep, that not only kept the grass looking great, but fertilized it in the process. When I first married, I fantasized that each spring I'd buy a lamb for ten dollars. That lamb would then cut and fertilize my lawn all summer. When fall came, I would barbecue the lamb and invite all my friends and neighbors to a party. They would, of course, feel obligated to invite us over to dinner later. I figured I could eat all winter and relax all summer thanks to that ten-dollar investment. Alas, my wife didn't think having a sheep tethered in the front lawn would look respectful.

What *appears* to be the simplest solution seldom is. It would appear that contacting a teenager in the area would solve all your problems. However, from experience, I've found that teenagers are less reliable than adults. (Teenagers who wish to protest may write to me at the address in the back of the book.) The reasons have to do with motivation. The teenager you hire to maintain your lawn already has parents, a place to live, food, and pocket money. If he does not show up at the scheduled time, he will not suffer eviction, starvation, or harassment by creditors. An adult who earns his living by selling lawn-maintenance services has to worry about all of these. A teenager has other things, such as school, dating, hanging out with friends, etc., that will take priority over your lawn care. An adult is doing this for a living, which ceases when customers cease to be happy. An adult, statistically, is far more likely to show up regularly than a teenager.

Therefore, if you want someone who will do what he promises, when he promises, time after time after time, go for an adult. Strangely, I've found that there isn't much difference in the prices, either. Perhaps that is because teenagers, who tend to work at will, have a most exaggerated idea of what labor goes for in America. Also, teenagers usually want to use *your* equipment—adults usually bring their own.

If, like me, you hate yard work but love beautiful lawns, here's how to go about finding your own lawn-care professional.

TIPS AND TACTICS

1. Ask friends.

If you're unconvinced by my logic on hiring teenagers, you can even ask those friends who hire teenagers to cut their lawns. Don't bother asking those who rely upon their *own* teenagers to cut their lawns. (These friends can be identified by the tall, flowering weeds in their front lawn.)

2. Ask for references.

Before you commit yourself to a schedule of maintenance, ask other customers about reliability and completeness. One teenager we hired was going to cut, edge, and weed-eat the lawn, and sweep off the patio and sidewalk every other Saturday. That happened once in a row. When we got tired of calling him on Monday and asking, "Where were you Saturday?" he said, "Well, I'll come out about *every ten days*." I realized that this was three times a month instead of the agreed-upon two times a month, but I acquiesced. He didn't come every ten days, of course. He came sporadically. However, his first bill showed four mowings. We didn't think he had come that often, but we paid the bill and started marking on the calendar when he had been there. The next month, we also got a bill for four mowings. (By this time, the facade about the trimming, edging, and sweeping had long since been forgotten!) We presented him with evidence that he had only been there three times. He went out to the pickup and came back a couple of minutes later with

a handwritten schedule showing four cuttings. Ironically, even though we had only a half inch of rain in two
months, he showed that one cutting followed another by
just four days! Moral: Get references.

3. Ask how long they've been in the business.

A lot of people get into lawn care when they've been laid
off from another job and will be doing it only until they
find full-time employment again. If your lawn-care professional has been in business for two years or more,
chances are he is committed to the profession and will
continue to be there when you need him.

4. Ask what's included in the price.

When you compare prices, be certain that you are also
comparing services. One fee might simply include lawn
mowing, another might also include edging, blowing off
walks and patio, checking sprinkler systems, keeping
hedges trimmed, etc. If you prefer to do some of these
things yourself, make certain that you get the price for
full service first, and then negotiate a lower price for just
what you want.

5. Observe them in action.

Before you sign any contracts, make any promises, etc.,
ask them to come out and "do" your lawn once. If you are
told, "We only work under contract," ask where they are
working, so you can go and see them in action. You
should find:

- their equipment in good repair (Dull mower blades do
  not cut grass evenly.)
- they show respect for property (I just hate it when I

have to go out and reattach drain pipe extensions that were knocked off by riding mowers, repair damaged flower bed borders, close gates left open, etc.)

6. *Ask about the lawn-care products they use.*
Fertilizers, herbicides, fungicides, and pesticides are specific and somewhat regional. Make certain that the products they use are right for your problem and your area—and not appreciably more expensive than they would be if you purchased them yourself. If their products are considerably more than you could purchase them for or if they prefer a chemical approach and you prefer a natural approach, ask what they would charge to apply your lawn chemicals.)

SUMMARY AND CONCLUSION

Not all lawns are the same size or of the same complexity. When we lived in Dallas, we had a quarter-acre lot (10,890 square feet). When you deducted 2,600 square feet for house and patio, 800 square feet for alley easement, 600 square feet for driveway, and 75 square feet for sidewalk, you were looking at a mere 6,800 square feet available for lawn and flowers. It does *not* take a lot of effort, experience, or equipment to handle a lawn of that size.

However, when we moved to Mineola, we had an acre lot, which left us with 39,485 square feet, or approximately nine-tenths of an acre to care for, which required more extensive knowledge and equipment. When we moved to Georgetown, we acquired a two-and-one-half-acre lot, which, after deducting for house, patio, and drive, leaves us in the neighborhood of 103,150 square feet for which to care. We are now talking about a heavy commitment of manpower and equipment.

The point is, the more you have to do, the more important it becomes that everything be done properly. If a lawn-care professional overapplied fertilizer and the grass began to die in my tiny backyard in Dallas, a hundred square yards of St. Augustine grass would replace the entire area. If a lawn-care professional makes the same mistake on my current lawn, we're talking of a catastrophe of biblical proportions. In other words, the wrong action by the wrong person could easily negate decades of savings, so make certain that the person you hire knows what he is doing!

How important is your lawn to you? Once you've answered that, you'll have a good idea how much time and research to put into finding just the right lawn-care professional to help you take care of it!

Locksmith

Locks are nothing new. During the excavation of ancient Nineveh, they found a four-thousand-year-old lock that used pins similar to modern locks! In the four hundred decades that have passed since then, locks have become more complex, stronger, and, judging by today's crime statistics, more necessary.

Before we get into locks, we need to give some definitions. There are three major types of locks.

- Rim locks go on the surface of a door or drawer.
- Mortise locks go into a precut cavity.
- Portable locks, like padlocks, are not permanently attached.

On exterior doors, we are most likely to find:

- a night latch, which is a lock with the bolt tapered on the side facing out so that it moves back into the lock as the door is closed. Once the door is closed, a spring pushes the bolt out into a predrilled cavity, and the door cannot be opened from the outside. At least, that's the theory. As any reader of detective fiction knows, it's a simple task to slip a thin piece of metal or plastic between the door and the jamb, and move the bolt back into the lock and open the door.

  - a dead bolt which has a square bolt that must

be thrown manually once the door is closed. It can only be opened from the outside with a key.

Whenever you move into a new home or apartment, you should have your locks changed by a competent locksmith. Also, if you do not have dead bolts on all your outside doors, you should have them installed to increase your security. If you have a sliding glass door, that will be your weakest link. Most can be readily lifted out of the frame and those that can't, in order to conform to safety regulations, have to break into granules upon impact. Therefore, a burglar with a BB gun can walk right in.

Here's how to find a good locksmith in your area.

TIPS AND TACTICS

1. Check the Yellow Pages.
Look for a locksmith that is both *bonded* and *insured*. (*Bonded* means the employees have been fingerprinted and investigated. *Insured* means you are covered for any damage they might do, such as ruin your new door, or walk off with your silver service.)

2. Look for time-in-grade.
Look for a locksmith who's been in business for several years. While that does not necessarily mean that the person he sends to your home has tenure, it at least means that the owner is in business to stay and has a dedicated interest in keeping customers happy.

3. Look for memberships in trade organizations.
ALOA (Associated Locksmiths of America) provides information to help members run a successful business

and is a self-policing organization dedicated to ensuring high standards of ethics and service. A locksmith who is interested in continually improving service and performance might belong to this as well as state and local organizations. If a locksmith doesn't belong to one of these trade organizations, it doesn't mean he isn't qualified and highly ethical. But belonging is a plus.

4. Look for locksmiths who take credit cards.

Should you have a problem later, such as one of the locks that was re-keyed doesn't accept the new key and the locksmith isn't interested in fixing the problem, you can appeal to the credit card company and withhold payment. And never, never, never pay for services before they are rendered.

5. Call the leading contenders.

They should be professional, courteous, and friendly. They should also be able to quote prices over the telephone. Don't be afraid to compare prices.

6. Don't admit any locksmith who makes you feel uncomfortable.

Learn to listen to those warning voices you hear!

7. Make certain that you agree on what is to be done before he begins.

Don't be surprised by a hole drilled in your front door for a lock when you *assumed* he was going to just use the hole occupied by the old lock.

8. Know your locks as well as your locksmith.

If you're buying replacement locks, ask several locksmiths which are the most durable and reliable. However, remember that a lock is only a *deterrent* to a break-in. A determined thief *will* get into your house, either by forcing the door or a window. Don't think that just because you purchase the highest-priced lock ever made you are necessarily buying more security. Be a wise shopper.

9. *Never again use a locksmith who:*

- provides "lock-out" service yet doesn't ask you for identification (To protect the public, a reputable locksmith will require you to show identification before unlocking a home or car for you, because, for all he knows, you could be a burglar.)
- does sloppy work or leaves a mess in your home
- tries to charge more than estimated without giving a valid reason
- asks you to pay in advance

SUMMARY AND CONCLUSION

When researching locksmiths, we learned that the term "master locksmith," at least in Texas, means absolutely nothing. Anyone may call himself a master locksmith. We also learned that chain latches on your doors provide virtually no protection at all. Oh, the chains themselves are strong, but 99 percent of the time you're screwing them into a piece of half-inch molding that's held on to a stud by six finishing nails. A good shove and the molding comes off, and the monster comes in. Dead bolts provide the best protection, but only if you don't open the door when a stranger rings your bell. (There is no rule of etiquette requiring you to open the door to everyone who knocks or rings!) If you want protection once the door is ajar, you'll need a strong chain with screws long enough to burrow into the door frame itself.

Since courts can't, or won't, keep criminals locked up, we have to lock up ourselves. Follow the instructions here, and you should have no problems.

Mail Service

OVERVIEW

Back in 1976, when I began writing full-time, I worked at home. Life was uncomplicated then; I just had another line installed in a spare bedroom, and I was all set. After all, no one ever went to my office; I went to theirs, and they didn't care where I worked. To keep business and personal mail from merging, I rented a box at the local post office and had my business mail sent there. What could be simpler?

Everything worked as planned except separating the business and personal mail. When you write sales, training, and safety programs for business and industry, deadlines fly like Frisbees on the first day of spring, and people need to get things to you immediately, if not sooner. In an attempt to beat normal mail delivery, clients began inundating me with packages delivered by UPS, Emery Air Freight, Federal Express, Airborne, etc. If my wife and/or I weren't going to the door to accept a delivery for me, we were going to the door to accept one for a neighbor. It became very, very difficult to work without interruption.

I solved the problem by renting a box at a mail service. Since they called my box a "suite," I suddenly had a very prestigious-sounding address.

I liked it so well that I had new letterheads, envelopes, and business cards printed, and listed the "suite number" and the street address of the mail service and gave my business line number at home. That way, when packages were delivered, there was someone to sign for them, and I could pick them up at *my* convenience, not at the convenience of the carrier. Soon I was having all my business mail delivered there. When I moved from Dallas to Mineola, a hundred miles from my nearest client, I kept the "suite" and teasingly told my clients that now they had "one great writer in two great locations."

Mail services are very, very beneficial to small businesses, like mine. But they are just as beneficial to home owners who simply have no one at home during the day. When *you* have a package, one of two unacceptable things can happen:

1. You come home and find a yellow sticky-note saying that they attempted delivery and that you can call and they'll try again.

2. Your package is set on your doorstep, telling any thief passing by that there's a free gift outside and that more are available inside—since it's obvious that no one is home.

Think about having your package safe and available on the day it arrives, ready and waiting for you to pick up at your convenience. As Eliza Doolittle asked in *My Fair Lady*, "Wouldn't it be loverly?"

"But wait," you say, "that means I'll have to get mail at two locations—at home and at the mail service!" Well, you could continue to get your mail at home and just give the address of your mail service for your packages. But if you're like me and have a fairly new home, you don't get your mail at home anyway. I live in a neighborhood of twenty-five-hundred- to four-thousand-square-foot homes on two-and-a-half to five-acre lots. Yet, we don't get mail service to our homes like the folks in the trailer park do. We have to drive nearly two miles to a rusted "United States Post Office Cluster Box," which sits out in an area surrounded by tall grass, old tires, old trash, and for all I know, muggers and monsters. *If I'm going to have to drive to get any of my mail, I figure it would be nice to get it all at the same location!* A nice location, with air conditioning, people, and lights.

If you feel you'd benefit by having someone there Monday through Saturday to receive (or send) your mail and packages, here's how to find a good mail service!

TIPS AND TACTICS

1. Look for one that's convenient.
Your service should be close to your office or your home, which will make it easier for you to pick up and send packages.

2. Look for one that's going to be there.
When we lived in Mineola, Texas, someone put in a mail service in a Wal-Mart Super Center. Since the Walton family is worth about $8.5 billion and they had decided to build a twenty-thousand-square-foot store in a town of forty-three hundred, I naturally assumed that everything

was there to stay. Wrong. The mail service lasted just a couple of months. *Fortunately,* I had not found time to reprint my letterhead, envelopes, and business cards!

If you don't want your mail service to be gone before the ink is dry on your contract, get one with tenure. Talk to them beforehand; ask if there's a living in what they do and if they want to stay in the business, etc.

3. Look for one that offers shipping options.

My mail service will take a receipt from any carrier and will ship my packages out by regular U.S. Mail, Express Mail, UPS, and Federal Express. Make certain yours offers *your* favorite outbound shipper.

4. Look for extra services.

Just about all mail services offer stamps, envelopes, labels, boxes, and tape. Some also offer office supplies, photocopying, greeting cards, gift items, and even gift wrap! My service in Georgetown does all of that, plus they'll wrap, package, and ship items for me, sell me insurance if I want it, and even forward my mail while I'm on vacation. One mail service we know routinely handles mass mailings for their customers, sells gifts, gift wraps things you buy there or bring in from other stores, and then packages everything up and ships it!

5. Look for one that works with you.

Overnight delivery of an eight-ounce parcel can cost up to $7.50 more than following-day delivery, and if it *doesn't* get there, you can get your money back—if you're patient, persistent, and persevering. Is it worth it? Your mail service can help you decide—and can also give you advice from personal experience as to which service *tradition-ally* offers the best service to the city you're shipping to!

6. Realize they're in business to make a profit.

Most of us in business are nice people. However, practically none of us are in business just to be nice people. Therefore, realize that, in addition to making a profit on your box rental, they are probably going to mark up everything they do. For instance, when I come into my mail service with $2.90 postage on a priority-mail package, they take it and mail it for me. If I come in with the same parcel and they weight it and sell me the stamps, they're going to charge me $3.50. That's fine. However, if I had ten packages to go out, I'd buy some stamps at the U.S. Post Office and mail the packages there.

Reasonable charges are fine, but call the U.S. Post Office, Federal Express, UPS, and the other services, and find out what the base charges are. Then you can decide whether the service your mail service offers is worth the surcharge.

SUMMARY AND CONCLUSION

In the last fifteen years, I've had three mail services. One was brief, but horrible; one was wonderful; and the one I have now is very good. The one that was horrible was staffed by people who, obviously, belonged to the Do-Nothing Society, and it collapsed as quickly as it opened, although with much less fanfare and notice. The one that was wonderful was in Dallas. The man who ran the service would even open my mail and read it to me or tell me if a check was inside! The one I have now is more for-mal, but very reliable.

A mail service gives a small business, such as mine, a permanent street address where someone is always pre-sent to receive packages. In addition, even when we could receive packages, it is nice to be able to work with-out interruption. By using the mail service, I get my packages when it is convenient.

A mail service can be an even bigger benefit to those who live in today's "nuclear family," when no one is home to receive packages during the day. With mail ser-vice, the catalog item or gift you were expecting will be accepted by someone you can trust and who can even call and tell you it's in!

The unanswered question is, "Do I go with a franchise or an independent operation?" We could find no divid-ing line there. Those who were franchise operations, of course, believed that was the way to go. Those who weren't, didn't. A franchise operation takes a piece of the action and provides training and a certain degree of name recognition. However, handling your mail and re-ceiving your packages, while vitally important, doesn't exactly require a degree in rocket science, and the only advantage a nationally advertised name has is that it might make you stop there instead of somewhere else. So, the advertising is for their benefit, not yours.

Many mail services belong to the Associated Mail and Parcel Centers, which provides training, but generally concentrates on ways to improve business by increasing volume. That's good, because a successful business will stay in business, and you won't have to look for a new place anytime soon. But again, the benefit of membership is geared more to the owner than to the customer.

In retailing, they say the three most important ingredients for success are:

1. location
2. location
3. and location

If I were you, and I wanted someone to receive my packages and/or mail, I'd go for the one with the best location, and if there were more than one service that was convenient, I'd go for the one which made me feel the most secure about the future of its business and offered the most service at the lowest price.

Massage Therapist

OVERVIEW

Anyone can give you a massage, and any massage, such as a good back rub, can be soothing and relaxing. However, massage *therapy* can only be administered by someone who has received intensive training. The therapist strokes, compresses, and kneads tissues to promote circulation and muscle tone, reduce swelling, soften scars, relieve muscle stiffness and fatigue, and increase the range of motion. *That* kind of massage, which can be called a Swedish massage, a deep muscle massage, or stress therapy and relaxation massage, is so beneficial that physicians and chiropractors often refer their patients to massage therapists to get it.

Now that you know the difference between a *massage* and *massage therapy*, you understand that a massage therapist never works in a massage *parlor.* "Massage parlor" is sometimes an euphemism for something quite different, and any time you see an ad for "massage" adjacent to a row of sleazy bars or grouped with the X-rated movie ads in the newspapers, you can be almost totally certain that you won't find a registered massage therapist on staff! Unfortunately, the publishers of the Yellow Pages lump them all together. Pick up any metropolitan telephone book and turn to "Massage" and you'll find ads for registered massage therapists right alongside those with no credentials at all or credentials that don't sound credible, such as those offering modeling and massage or those boasting sexy-sounding names or names with a double entendre built in. (If *you* think it's frustrating, you should hear the registered massage therapists complain!)

Here's how to find someone who gives a medically approved massage!

TIPS AND TACTICS

1. Find the genuine article.
Whether you're acting on a lead from a friend or picking someone out of the telephone book, look for the initials "MT" (massage therapist) or "RMT" (registered massage therapist) and a license number. RMTs might also list organizations to which they belong, such as AAMT (American Association of Massage Therapists), or ABWP (Association of Body Work Professions). While requirements vary by state, in Texas, a licensed or "registered" massage therapist must successfully complete a minimum of three hundred classroom hours of instruction including anatomy, physiology, kinesiology, business ethics, and interpersonal skills. (You can check your state's requirements by calling the state licensing board or any RMT in the telephone book.)

2. Find the right atmosphere.
Visit the office of a therapist. You should find the atmosphere quiet, relaxing, clean, and professional, with the waiting room separate from the treatment room, and no more than one patient in any treatment room.

3. Ask for references.

Most therapists will be happy to give you names of patients and/or physicians, chiropractors, or orthopedic surgeons with whom they work.

4. Find the right massage therapist.

On your first visit, after taking your case history and giving a massage, a good therapist will know if the problem is something he can treat or if you need a referral. If not, he will proceed. Massage therapy requires strength, stamina, and endurance. If your therapist has it, you'll probably get a full hour's worth of massage therapy. If he doesn't, he might visit with you for ten or fifteen minutes to use up some of the therapy time. Your therapist should not, except in an emergency, leave to take telephone calls, and most of those we interviewed feel that they can do a better job if they don't engage you in conversation while they work.

Massage therapists are involved primarily in decreasing pain and increasing the range of motion through deep muscle massage. I'd be uncomfortable if the therapist talked about things like "tracer work," or any other technique that promised to do massage without touching. Tracer work, like UFO sightings, elicits strong comments, both pro and con, but I personally prefer physical massage, and I personally know of no physicians who recommend the nontouching variety.

SUMMARY AND CONCLUSION

I'm fortunate in having a sister-in-law who's a registered

massage therapist, so I know firsthand how beneficial a deep muscle massage can be. The fact that I fell and injured my back a few years ago, and spend ten to twelve hours a day hunkered down and slaving over a hot word processor, does nothing for my posture or my muscle tone. Yet, after one of her treatments, I feel younger, more alert, and I stand taller.

If you're not fortunate enough to have a registered massage therapist in your family, following these instructions will help you find one. If you *do* have one in your family, following the instructions will give you a basis for comparison!

Minor Emergency Center

OVERVIEW

You see them everywhere, the little signs in strip shopping centers that say, "Minor Emergency Center," "Minor Emergency Clinic," or just "Minor Emergency." I used to drive by and wonder, "What constitutes a *minor* emergency?" I decided it must be when *you* break *your* leg. When I break *my* leg, it's a *major* emergency!

Since most Americans work Monday through Friday, the weekends would be a great time to go to the doctor for routine checkups, colds, vaccinations, and all the other things we need that we can't take off during the week to have done. Also, we are more likely to be injured on the weekend, which means it is also the time we're most likely to need emergency health care. Unfortunately, doctors take the same days off we do, so their offices are closed on weekends. All this makes one wonder what would happen if other professions followed the example of doctors and closed on *their* busiest days. That would mean that amusement parks, theaters, and restaurants would be closed on weekends. Synagogues would close on Saturdays. Churches would close on

Sundays! TV networks wouldn't broadcast during prime time.

Because doctors take off on weekends, we must somehow schedule routine medical matters during the week. But what about unscheduled events—such as "minor" emergencies? Well, since your doctor is off, your traditional choice was a hospital emergency room. However, in recent years, "Minor Emergency" operations have been cropping up in shopping malls and strip shopping centers, offering a place to go. Because they are convenient, some people go there, not only for emergencies, but also for routine things such as vaccinations, or for a physical or a cold.

By the time we got around to interviewing minor emergency center staffers, my staff and I had conducted well over two hundred interviews. Therefore, we had our presentations down pat: explaining what I do for a living, the topics of recent books I'd authored or coauthored, the scope of this book, and the professions we were covering. We'd then say, "We'd like to ask you the same question we asked attorneys, dentists, doctors, chiropractors, builders, bankers, and other professionals: 'What would you look for if you were looking for someone in your business? That is, if you were out of town and needed to go to a minor emergency center, what would *you* look for?"

The presentation and questions were straightforward, delivered in the same manner as we had used in garnering information for the other sixty-three professions covered in this book. Ironically, at each minor emergency center, *everyone clammed up and wouldn't talk with us*! *This included a minor emergency center where Michael, John Morin's son, had been a patient!* When pressed, management at each of the seven minor emergency centers we visited seemed to become nervous and apprehensive. The most common excuse for not answering our question was, "For all we know, you could be *attorneys* or *competitors.*" We presented proof of the book and on two occasions even presented the "Overviews," "Tips and Tactics," and "Summaries and Conclusions" for other professions. We repeated, "The purpose of this book is to enable people to find a *good banker, a good dentist, a good auto repairman, a good doctor, and a good minor emergency center.*" Some promised to get back with us. None did.

Since all my books have been very pro-business and we had not met with this kind of resistance in any other field, we couldn't help wondering why 100 percent of those sampled exhibited an almost paranoid fear that we were trying to get something on them. Could this unanimous rejection be merely a coincidence? Possibly, but this writer feels that this much fear must be fueled by facts. Lacking knowledge as to what those facts might be and receiving no help from those who operate such facilities *even so much as providing a definition of "minor emergency,"* I have determined to never, never, never enter such a facility. You, of course, should decide for yourself.

TIPS AND TACTICS

None

SUMMARY AND CONCLUSION

If you have a "minor emergency," go to your own physician or the nearest hospital emergency room. They not only have the staff to treat you, but should your opinion of a "minor emergency" turn out to be something they would call a "major emergency," they can provide whatever level of care you might need. And they won't be afraid of your questions!

Nursing Home

OVERVIEW

It was autumn and my aged grandparents lived in a little house in the deep East Texas woods all by themselves. My grandmother was getting forgetful, and my grandfather, a retired lawman who was once able to set up kitchen matches on a split-rail fence and strike them by shooting at them from twenty-five feet with a government-issue .45 handgun, was nearly blind and almost totally deaf. The family was afraid that, with approaching winter, my grandmother would turn on the gas in the space heaters, forget to light it, and that they'd asphyxiate. Therefore, they asked me to convince them to check into a nursing home for the winter.

There is a great deal of relief when a family gets together and makes a tough decision. Unfortunately, that relief is seldom shared by the one asked to carry out the decision and actually "bell the cat." However, I eventually talked my grandparents into going and moved them in for the brief couple of months of winter we have here in Texas. It was both physically and emotionally exhausting.

When I got home, one of my sisters called me and asked, "Well, how did they feel about it?"

I thought a moment and replied,

"They felt about it just as you or I would have. They're no different from us—*just older.*"

If you are seeking a nursing home, I know what you're going through. If you're wondering what your aged relatives think about the idea, well, they're thinking the same thoughts you would be thinking. They don't want to go.

Socrates said, "All men would live long, but none would be old." In this era of scattered families with both spouses working, few are able to take care of aged parents (or grandparents) when they can no longer care for themselves. This means that you must either find someone willing to live in and do it, which is virtually impossible, or find a good nursing home.

There are great nursing homes, good nursing homes, and what I call "kennels," those which barely scrape by the state standards. Our daughter, who loves elderly people, once worked as a nurse's aide in one of the latter. She was constantly getting into trouble because she refused to feed residents in the required five minutes. She tried to explain that even *she* couldn't eat in five minutes and was told the secret was to get between two beds and to offer one bed patient a bite, and while he chewed it, to offer a bite to the other patient. Rebecca explained that even she couldn't eat in *ten* minutes and that many of the bed patients had trouble chewing or swallowing. Many times, she came home in tears after catching flack for doing what was right rather than what she was told to do. This same administrator would virtually lose control if one of the normal, ragged blankets wound up in the front wing where most visitors came.

Years after checking my grandparents into a nursing home for that single winter, my grandfather died, and my grandmother moved into a nursing home near us. This was one of the finest facilities I've seen anywhere. The staff, the nurses, and the aides laughed and joked and visited with her when she was able to respond, and, as her Alzheimer's disease advanced to the point where she no longer recognized any of us, even moments after we were introduced, they continued to talk with her and to provide her with the same level of care a loving family would have provided had they been able.

Our personal experience with nursing homes, coupled with the knowledge gained by asking administrators, "What would *you* look for if you were looking for a good nursing home?" gives me confidence that you'll find what you need if you'll follow these tips and tactics.

TIPS AND TACTICS

1. Get qualified recommendations.
A qualified recommendation would be:
- your relative's physician (although not all physicians will make nursing home visits)
- a physician you respect
- ministers
- a friend who has a relative or acquaintance in a nursing home

the board of health (Just call and ask for a list of the top five facilities in your area.)

2. *Make several unannounced visits at different times to the top homes on your list.*

Sunday, when most relatives visit residents, is not a good day for your inspection, as even the worst homes will be spic-and-span then. Drop by on a weekday at midmorning, midafternoon, or right after dinner in the evening. You should find:

- clean, well-landscaped, attractive grounds
- a clean, odor-free interior
- a homelike atmosphere in intermediate-care facilities
- recreational activities suitable to the capabilities of the residents
- organized activities, with a monthly calendar of events
- a hospital-like atmosphere in intensive-care facilities
- well-groomed, well-mannered, well-trained, friendly staff who take time to talk with the patients and know them by name

3. *Stop and chat with alert residents.*

In every facility, you will find that *some* of the residents have lost their faculties. However, this is by no means always the case. Many are there simply because they are no longer *physically* able to take care of themselves, and are still mentally alert and quite sharp. No, no one will think you're being nosy! Most nursing homes and virtually all residents love to have visitors. Some go months without an outside visitor.

Rebecca tells of one elderly lady who got all dressed up on Mother's Day, knowing her children, who she had not seen in three months, would come then. She waited first with anxious anticipation, and then with steadily diminished hope as the day gave way to evening. Not a call. Not a card. Nothing. And the woman was alert and lively, and an interesting conversationalist. No, they won't consider you an intruder. They will consider you a friend. Ask them what they like about the place and what they don't like. Understand, of course, that they would prefer to be home with their own things, and their own friends, and their own family . . . even as you and I.

4. Visit with the staff.

Visit with everyone from the floor nurse, to the charge nurse, to nurse's aides. Ask them what they like about the facility and what they would like to see changed.

5. Visit with any family members who might be visiting relatives.

Family members can give you the "lowdown" on what really goes on, what they like and don't like, and what they'd like to see changed.

6. Visit with the administrator.

Explain that you are looking for a facility for a loved one and ask him to tell you about his facility. During this conversation you should:

- pick up a brochure, if one is available
- find out about rates
- obtain a copy of the activity calendar
- ask if they take Medicare when funds are depleted

- obtain a copy of the last inspection by the board of
  health

SUMMARY AND CONCLUSION

In the facility where my grandmother lived out her last
Alzheimer-dazed days, there was a sign in the nurses'
break room that said, "Remember, our residents do not
make their homes where we work, we work in their
homes." That is a wonderful attitude for a nursing home
to have.

If you really want the nursing home you choose to
seem like home to the loved one you're placing there,
visit, send cards, write, telephone. Take him out for
shopping sprees and lunches, and invite him to your
home on holidays. Let him know that you still love him,
and involve your children in the selection process and
the visits. After all, someday *we* will be old, and what our
children see us do for our parents, they will do for us.

Nutritionist

OVERVIEW

When I was a child, at the end of each meal, my mother would look at my plate and say, "Marcus, eat your green beans! Children in Southeast Asia are starving!" When I grew up, I wound up in Vietnam where the now-grown children in Southeast Asia were shooting at me. When this happened, I always wanted to jump up and yell, "Hey, show some respect! *I'm* the guy who ate those awful canned green beans for you!"

While I didn't (and don't) care for canned green beans, my mother did instill in me the importance of the basic four food groups. And that's good, because, "You are," as the old saw goes, "what you eat."

Knowledge of nutrition has cured many of the ancient diseases that once plagued mankind, and today one seldom hears of rickets, pellagra, scurvy, or goiter. We have learned much, but there is still much to be learned. Most of us realize that, just as small amounts of medicines our physicians prescribe affect us, so do the much larger amounts of foods we eat. The things we eat, as well as the *things we do not eat,* can help or hurt our health. This has always been true, but today, our bodies have the added burden of stress, and the fast-food fodder that our fast-paced lives cause us to eat leaves us nutritionally disadvantaged.

Good nutritional advice is important to everyone, particularly those among us who face chronic health problems. Yet, finding a source of good personalized nutritional advice can be challenging in spite of the number of ads you'll find in the Yellow Pages under "nutrition." According to Michael Schiferl of the American Dietetic Association, just about anyone can call himself a nutritionist. (See entries under "Electrician," "Financial Planning," and "Massage Therapist.") In fact, a recent edition of the *Tufts University Diet and Nutrition Letter*[29] states that a survey of telephone directories in thirty-two states indicated that less than half of the so-called professionals listed under the heading of "nutritionists" and "physicians" are reliable sources of sound, scientifically based nutrition information.

According to the same article, "Some 70 percent of the nutritionist 'Ph.D.'s' listed in the Yellow Pages, for example, sport phony degrees or deliver fraudulent information. Others carry self-proclaimed titles such as certified nutritionist (CN), doctor of nutrimedicine (NMD), nutrition counselor (NC), or myriad other illegitimate credentials. Confusing the matter further is the fact that such practitioners often tout 'degrees' from reputable-sounding institutions . . .which award so-called diplomas even though they've not been accredited."

....

[29] July 1994

Ira Milner, RD, author of the Yellow Pages survey and coordinator of the Task Force for Nutrition Diploma Mills for the National Council Against Health Fraud, says that many states lack a system for regulating the parlaying of nutrition information, so that anyone can claim to be a nutritionist without fear of legal recourse. He finds no cases that were taken to court, although he does cite the case of one quack dispensing expensive, potentially harmful, nutrition information who was fined $250.

How do you find a *genuine* nutritionist article, the real diamond in a field of zircons? Follow the guidelines below!

TIPS AND TACTICS

1. Begin with a registered dietitian (RD).
Such a person will have *at least* a bachelor of science degree from a college or university accredited by the American Board of Medical Specialties, will have served as an intern in a hospital or other coordinated program, and will have passed a national examination. While nondegreed people calling themselves "nutritionists" usually escape punishment, RDs are not only educationally qualified, but in thirty-four states and Puerto Rico, they will be licensed. (In Texas, licensed RDs also carry the designation "LD" [licensed dietitian]. The designation RD lets you know that the person talking to you really knows what he's talking about.)

2. Look for membership in the ADA.
The American Dietetic Association, with more than sixty-four thousand members, is the largest group of food and

nutrition professionals in the nation. Three-fourths of the members are RDs, with the balance made up of educators, researchers, dietetic technicians, registered dietetic technicians (DTRs), and students. Incidentally, according to the ADA, 63 percent of the RDs working in hospitals have advanced degrees, making them, as a group, second only to physicians in educational level!

3. Look for someone with expertise in your area of concern.

ADA membership covers a wide range of practice areas and special interests, including:

- allergies
- cardiovascular disease and hypertension
- cholesterol reduction
- diabetes
- digestive disorders
- eating disorders
- education of other health-care professionals
- food-service management in:
  - business
  - hospitals
  - schools
  - long-term-care facilities
  - education systems
- general nutrition and wellness
- gerontology (aging, Alzheimer's, arthritis)
- home health
- maternal and child health (pregnancy, childhood, adolescent)

- oncology (cancer, chemotherapy, AIDS)
- research
- sports nutrition
- vegetarian
- weight control

4. Look for other credentials.

If your concern is clinical nutrition, the International and American Associations of Clinical Nutritionists award CCNs (Certified Clinical Nutritionist) to those who have passed a rigorous test on the knowledge and practice of clinical nutrition.

5. Check 'em out.

Call your state board of health to check on licensing requirements. (Many RDs list their license number in their Yellow Page ads.) You may also call the American Dietetic Association at 1-800-877-1600, or the International and American Associations of Clinical Nutritionists, and ask for referrals of qualified members *in your area* who specialize in your area of need.

6. Call 'em up.

Call and ask if the nutritionist is an RD or a CCN. Ask where he went to school, how many hours were required, what his area of specialty is, and what his experience has been with your area of interest.

SUMMARY AND CONCLUSION

The ADA says that next to smoking and drinking, diet has the largest impact on our health. Today, one hears many different nutrition songs from many different singers, reminding one of the old American proverb, "A man with a watch always knows what time it is. A man with two watches is never certain!" Today, there are many nutrition voices crying to be heard from both re- spected and suspected quarters. How do you find your way through the nutrition maze? One of the best ways I know is call the experts at the number I just gave you. After all, the phone call is free, and the advice could be invaluable.

Optometrist

Optometrists, or "eye doctors," as we used to call them back in the prehistoric days of my childhood, prescribe over two-thirds of the eyewear in the United States. In order to become a Doctor of Optometry (O.D.), one must complete at least two years of preoptometry college work and graduate from a four-year school of optometry. The American Optometric Association definition of a therapeutically licensed optometrist is: *An independent primary health-care provider who examines, diagnoses, treats, and manages diseases and disorders of the visual system, the eye, and associated structures as well as diagnoses related systemic conditions.*

When do you need to see an optometrist? Whenever you have difficulty adjusting to darkness, focusing on near or far images, pain in or around your eyes, double vision, itching, burning, dryness, redness of the eyes, seeing halos or rainbows around lights, sensitivity to light, or a white or yellow appearance to the pupil. However, since diseases such as glaucoma can slowly, steadily, and permanently rob you of sight without any of these symptoms, it's a good idea to visit your optometrist for an eye exam at least once a year, even if you have none of the symptoms just mentioned.

Now that you know exactly what an optometrist does,

you might be wondering about a related profession: *ophthalmologist.* An opthamologist is an M.D. who limits his practice to the eye. He is medically trained to treat diseases of the eye with medication and/or surgery. Both an optometrist and an ophthalmologist are qualified to give you an eye examination and prescribe corrective lenses. So, which should you see? An optometrist will charge less for this service, and if you have a good one, he will refer you to an ophthalmologist should the situation warrant.[30]

TIPS AND TACTICS

Here's how to go about selecting your optometrist.

1. Ask for references.

If you're moving to a new area, ask your present O.D. to recommend a good optometrist where you'll be relocating. Also, ask your personal physician and friends who they use and recommend. Ask if the staff is friendly and well trained, if the doctor takes time to talk with you and listen to you, or if they feel rushed.

While I'd prefer to begin with a personal recommendation, you could call the AOA (American Optometric

....

[30] Several years ago, while sitting in a client's office, it suddenly looked as if a spider web had latched on to my left eyelashes. I excused myself, went to the rest room, but could find nothing on the outside of the eye to account for what I was seeing. I called my optometrist, Dr. Toby McClenny, and drove directly to his office. He examined the eye, saw what I called a "tethered floater" and said that the pressure was up in that eye and he was referring me to a specialist. I said, "That will take weeks, I know how they are." He said, "No, I'll get you in today!" and did! Since then, I have had every confidence that Dr. McClenny is in perfect control of my eye care—because if he doesn't know for certain that he can handle the problem, he doesn't mind referring me to someone who can. That's what being an "expert" is all about!

Association) or your state optometric association and ask them for a referral. The easiest way to do that is dial 1-800-555-1212 and ask if there's a toll-free listing.

When you have your recommendations, it's time to move to the next step in your quest.

2. Call a couple of clinics.

Explain that you are new to the area or have a problem and don't know an optometrist. Ask questions like these:

■ How long has the doctor been in practice? (You'll probably not prefer one who is just out of school or one who is about to retire.)

■ Ask if the doctor's equipment is up to date. (One optometrist we interviewed gave us quite a litany of equipment he said should be in a modern optometrist's office. The list was quite impressive to a guy who grew up in the 1950s and remembered an eye exam was an eye chart and a big face shield with a lot of lenses the doctor flipped while asking, "How does that look?" This doctor said the current standard of care testing would include:

  • computerized visual field testing for glaucoma patients
  • auto refractors for determining prescription
  • auto keratometers for measuring eye shape
  • gonioscopy for internal exam for glaucoma
  • tonometry for testing ocular pressure
  • fundus photographs or video imaging for pictures of the retina

- binocular and monocular indirect ophthalmoscopy for viewing inside the eye
- biomicroscopy for viewing anterior portions of the eye
- developmental vision testing and training for slow learners
- low-vision testing (use of special telescopes and high-powered magnifiers for very poor vision, such as macular degeneration)
- sport-vision testing, for improving perception, protection, and awareness
- corrected and noncorrected acuity testing (phoropter refraction to determine the glasses or contact lenses prescription)
- eye-muscle testing
- dilating the pupils for neurological evaluation
- gross examination of lid and facial structures

He also added that nonroutine special exam procedures would include:

- potential acuity meters for determining potential vision after cataract surgery
- visual-evoked responses
- ultrasound, including both A and B scan

Bear in mind that hundreds of tests are available during eye exams. Not all are necessary for every patient, but the doctor must have and use all that are needed to determine a diagnosis (the problem) and its etiology (what caused it.)

3. Visit a clinic.

If the staff put up with all your questions, kept their cool and allowed you to keep yours, visit them. Step inside and say, "I just came in to look around." See if the office is clean and well managed. If the staff is courteous and well mannered. If the reading material is reasonably current (don't you just love year-old news magazines?), and if there are large-type books and magazines for the visually impaired.

4. Make an appointment.

When you come in for your appointment, the staff or the doctor should take a very thorough case history which includes asking for all major complaints and all medications you take. During the exam, the doctor will probably:

- perform preliminary testing of the eyes to assess the shape, visual prescription, intraocular and blood pressure, before getting started with the internal and external examination of the eye itself
- be meticulous, careful, and confident (He should be a good explainer, telling you what he is doing and why. He should be a good listener, taking note of your questions and concerns. He should be a good communicator, giving you understandable examples and providing comfort and support.)

After the exam, the doctor should:

- be open to questions such as, "What is my problem?" "What is causing the problem?" "What can we do about it?"
- be able to answer your questions by saying:

- "This is the problem, this is what caused it, this is my recommended treatment, and this is the result you should expect."
- "I *believe* this is your problem and its cause, but I am not sure and would recommend further testing."
- "I don't know what your problem is, therefore I would like to refer you to a specialist."

SUMMARY AND CONCLUSION

My grandfather, who was a career peace officer with an eye so keen he could set up kitchen matches in a split-rail fence, back off twenty-five feet, and strike them with bullets from a government-issue .45 ACP handgun,[31] in his later years became one of the half-million Americans who lost his sight due to glaucoma. Sadly, in most cases, blindness due to glaucoma can be prevented if detected early through regular eye examinations! Because the changes came slowly, he waited until it was too late.

We need and cherish all of our senses, but to most of us the sense of sight is special. Ninety-five percent of all blindness is caused by disease—and many of these diseases are curable, or, like glaucoma, at least treatable if caught in time. How sad it would be if we allowed blindness to creep up on us because we were too busy to schedule an eye exam! To never again see the faces of those we love. To never see another sunset. To never see

....

[31] This amazing feat is only possible when the bullets come so close to the match heads that the heat caused by the friction of the passing bullet ignites the match!

children playing in the park, a favorite movie, or the vistas of this great land. Do yourself and your family a favor. If you have any of the symptoms described in this segment, or if you haven't had an eye exam in a couple of years, find an optometrist! Do it this week!

Painting Contractor

OVERVIEW

When the Bockmons buy a new home, I always make a list of things that are important. From time to time, in twenty-nine years of married life, the requirements have changed, but one item has made each and every list: *The house must not need painting.* I had rather fight a bear with a willow switch or do another tour of duty in Vietnam than paint a house.

Most of us don't do the things we hate very well, and when we do have an unpleasant chore to do, we try to get it over with as quickly as possible. In the immortal words of W. C. Fields, "There comes a time in every man's life when he must grab the bull by the tail and face the situation!" From time to time, I admit, I've been forced to grab the bull by the tail and paint. When those times have occurred, I went at the task like a banshee with a hyperactive thyroid.

I recall one painting experience when I only lacked one room and night was falling. Rather than face another sleepless night dreading the next day's painting, I decided to finish the task and be done with it. I turned on every light in the room and brought in other lights from other rooms. At last, about eleven o'clock, I looked on the room with pride, knowing that I had done great work in spite of the fact I hated doing it. I cleaned up the mess, turned off the lights, and went to bed.

When morning came, I went into the room and pulled the drapes so that I might admire my handiwork. To my horror, there were many missed places on the wall where the old paint showed through—and what a mess I'd left! While I would later make good use of this tale by explaining to my Sunday school class how our imperfections, like painting imperfections, might be hidden in dim light, but are all revealed in the light of God, no such thoughts were in my mind as I moved furniture back out, brought in the drop cloths, rollers, and buckets, sighed, and began again.

If, like me, you hate to paint and aren't very good at it, here's how to avoid having to grab the paintbrush by the tail and facing the situation yourself!

TIPS AND TACTICS

1. Check around.

- Ask friends who have recently hired painters. Ask what they liked and disliked about the work done. Ask if the painters were courteous, professional, punctual, and fair. Ask if the price originally quoted was the price actually paid. Ask if they cleaned up their mess when they were finished and hauled off their own trash.
- Ask your local paint-store manager: Tell him what kind of painting you need to have done, and ask him what the paint and other materials would cost. Then ask him to recommend a painter. Also, ask if the painter he is

recommending has an outstanding balance at the store. (I know of one case where a lumberyard recommended a handyman, not because he was good, which he wasn't, but because he owed them money, and they hoped he would use some of the money to pay his outstanding balance, which he didn't!)

■ Ask a good local builder or remodeler: They deal with a lot of painters, and can give you good advice on who to call—and who to avoid.

2. Always get at least three estimates.

I'd call the person my friend(s) recommended, the one the paint-store manager recommended, and a builder referral, and get estimates. From your visit to the paint store, you know about what the materials will run and will be able to compare prices on paint and labor.

While the contractor is there, ask:

■ Do you have a start-up cost? (Most painters ask for 25 percent up front, with the balance due upon completion. Never pay the balance until the work is completed.)

■ Do you have all the tools you need?

■ How many years' experience do you have?

■ What steps do you take prior to painting (caulking, pressure washing, priming, taping, etc.)?

■ Are you bonded and do you have liability insurance? (You do not want to have to pay for any injuries their workers might sustain, nor do you want to have to resort to hiring an attorney if they spill a half gallon of semigloss enamel paint on your prize Persian rug!)

■ Will you return to do touch-ups, cleanups, etc., on anything you might have missed?

3. Get references.

Sure, you got a reference from a friend, from a paint-store manager, and from a builder or remodeler, but that is *one in a row*. You want three to five references so you can make certain that the contractor routinely produces satisfied customers. References, of course, are of no value unless you take the time to call them. *Ideally, you take time to visit a couple of the references and actually see the work.* Finally, check the contractor through the Better Business Bureau.

4. Make certain the color you order is the color you want.

The color chips on a one-by-one-inch card are not always true, and colors look different in a store, under fluorescent lights, than they do outside under sunlight or in your home under incandescent lights. Before you commit a room or a house to an unusual color, have a sample painted, let it dry, and view it in what will be its natural habitat.

SUMMARY AND CONCLUSION

If you've read the overview and the tips and tactics, you should have no problem finding a good painter who will do the job promised on time and on budget. A few final words of caution: As much trouble and expense as painting is, you don't want to have to do it again for a long, long time. So make certain that you do three things.

First, get a good grade of paint, because cheap paint will require repainting much sooner than you might think. Second, make certain that the colors you get are the colors you really, really want. I remember my wife once picked out a shade of yellow she wanted in the kitchen. When I got it all painted, my wife came in and said, "Good Lord, it looks like the inside of a mustard jar! Would you repaint it?" The answer was, "Yes, but not *this* year." Third, realize that having painters underfoot will be a disruption to your life while the work is being done. (Just as having *you* underfoot will be a disruption to *his* life!) A little mutual patience and understanding will go a long way.

Avoid problems by picking the right painter, picking the right paint, and picking the right colors! And enjoy!

Photographer

OVERVIEW

Ever since George Eastman began selling cameras loaded with one hundred frames of film, we've been a nation of picture takers. In the old days, once you'd exposed all the film, you mailed the entire camera back to the factory, and they processed the prints and reloaded the camera! They've recently returned to their roots by selling cardboard-enclosed cameras with the film inside, that you send in when you've shot the last frame.

The cardboard camera notwithstanding, most cameras sold today are very sophisticated. In fact, more than one industrial photographer has lamented to me, "Ours is the only profession in the world where all the equipment is made for amateurs!" That's because there are thousands of amateur photographers for every professional, and camera designers and makers create a lot of nice "toys" so we can *somewhat* compensate for our lack of technical knowledge.

Consequently, today's electronic cameras automatically read the film speed on the film canister, then set the correct speed and exposure, focus, compute flash distance, and give you a green light or audible instructions when everything is ready. Press the button, the camera takes the picture, then automatically advances the film to the next shot. Finish the roll, and the camera even rewinds the film! Yet there is more to taking good photographs than taking a breath, letting half of it out, holding it, and pressing the shutter when the green light comes on.

Still, thanks to a combination of sophisticated equipment and a plethora of well-written photography books, some amateur photographers are very, very good. My friend Bill Hampton, who is a consultant and designer of computerized route distribution systems, is a good example. In fact, he is a much better available-light photographer than some professionals I know.

Professional, incidentally, merely means that one does it for a living. Some *professional* photographers know less about photography than some amateurs! I talked to one photographer who was setting up to do children's photos in a store for a couple of days, and all he really knew was that when he placed the lights, the subject, and the camera according to the chart, the photos would be properly exposed. The *professional* who shot the senior pictures for one of our daughters' yearbooks had 20 percent of them out of focus! When we wanted a portrait of her before her braces came off, those pictures were out of focus, too. (From a photographer that once worked for me, I learned that "out of focus" is called "soft focus" by professionals. He claimed the reason for the term was because *sometimes,* you could sell soft focus, but you could never sell a photo that you admitted was out of focus! He might have been teasing, however, as soft focus or "Doris Day lens" is often used in glamour photography.)

Still, while there are a few exceptionally good amateurs and a few exceptionally bad professionals, most photographers who make a full-time living at their trade will be much, much better than the best amateur. A good photographer will not only bring extra skill, judgment, and expertise to the project, but will also be able to "retouch" the photo so that the pimple that suddenly popped up on your nose the night before your photo session doesn't show. Also, professionals use better labs, so your negatives and prints will not only get modern electronic controls, but will be judged by practiced human eyes.

A professional portrait photographer seldom uses 35mm film, as larger film formats give crisper, clearer enlargements. (Incidentally, 35mm film was developed when Hollywood directors wanted to find a fast way to check lighting for motion pictures. They found that they could do this quickly and economically by using a still camera that used the same motion picture film they used, which, at that time, was 35mm!)

Since you might have need for both a personal and a commercial photographer, here are some tips and tactics for finding each.

TIPS AND TACTICS

PERSONAL PHOTOGRAPHY
1. Look for someone whose specialty is what you need.
If you want wedding photos, look for someone who

specializes in those. If you want your portrait taken in your home or outdoors, find out if your photographer is comfortable doing that or prefers to work in a studio. If you're looking for a wedding photographer, places that hold wedding receptions (churches, civic centers, country clubs, hotels, etc.) would be a good source of leads.

2. Check credentials.

Credentials are often mentioned in advertising. If not, they can be obtained over the telephone. Most good photographers will belong to a state or local organization which encourages growth among their members, such as the Texas Professional Photographers Association. In addition to state and local organizations, many professional photographers belong to the Professional Photographers of America (PPA). Although mere membership does not guarantee quality, membership establishes a standard for quality and service. The PPA also has a certification program that can result in a craftsman's or master's certificate. These certifications are difficult to obtain. The candidate must show that he has the necessary knowledge and experience, and he must pass a portfolio review board. Certifications, incidentally, must be renewed every five years.

3. Meet the photographer.

A photographer who works with people should have people skills. You don't want a surly, grouchy, noncommunicative, or dictatorial photographer taking your portrait, or ruining your wedding. Your photographer should act as if he's having a good time, too. If you're having a studio portrait made, the photographer should take the time to get to know you, understand your personality, and find out what portrait style you like.

3. Check his work.
A good photographer will be happy to show you his portfolio. Naturally, you will want to see samples of work similar to that you want done, i.e., formal, informal, interior, exterior, studio, home, backdrops, etc. Some photographers prefer an arty approach, while others are more traditional. Find someone whose style compliments your own taste and judgment.

4. Ain't nothin' free.
Beware of photographers who offer something for free. You may, if you are persistent, get the free item, but you'll usually have to resist a very slick, high-pressure sales presentation. If you're not careful, you'll wind up with poor photographs that cost you more than going to a reasonably priced, reputable photographer. Besides, some professional photographers have time pay plans and will work with you.

5. Once you've decided, trust your photographer.
Remember, the photographer can see you through the lens, but you can't see yourself. Therefore, trust his judgment when it comes to poses. After all, you're hiring an expert and much of that expertise is wasted if you don't heed the advice.

COMMERCIAL PHOTOGRAPHY
If your church, organization, service club, or business needs photography, you might need an entirely different

type of photographer—a *commercial* photographer. If you are needing an audio-visual presentation or a brochure, then you might need photos taken in difficult environments, such as factories, offices, assembly lines, or you might need "beauty" shots of the products you manufacture, distribute, or sell. Photographers who do this kind of work are frequently, but not always, found on staff at audio-visual production companies. They might also be found through the printers who do brochures. Here are some tips on how to find the right one for you.

1. Check the brochures used by local businesses.

When you see a style you like, call the marketing or public relations department and ask who the photographer was on that project.

2. Call a local quality printer.

Ask him to recommend a photographer who can do the kind of work you want.

3. Meet the photographer.

Although it isn't absolutely necessary that you have a rapport with an industrial photographer, if the "shooter" is going to be meeting and mixing with your employees, bosses, or co-workers, you don't want a jerk who barks orders or starts shooting without so much as a "May I?" or a "Do you mind?"

4. Check his work.

A good photographer will be happy to show you his portfolio. Naturally, you will want to see samples of work similar to what you want. Some industrial settings don't lend themselves to big lights or flash situations. If that's the case with your project, then you'll need someone who can work with the available light.

5. Explain the project.

If you describe what you want to accomplish and what you expect from the photography, a good photographer will tell you whether or not what you want is possible, and, if so, if he can do it.

6. Ask for references.

The best references, of course, will be those for whom he has done similar work.

7. Negotiate all fees in advance.

Today, many photographers copyright their work. This means that although you are paying for their time, for their skill, and for their film and processing, you do not own *all* rights to the photos unless and until you negotiate for them. Many a business has been chagrined to find that they received an extra bill when a photo they had made for a brochure wound up in one of their ads as well.

Others find that when they ask a photographer for twenty shots of an item, that the photographer might shoot twenty rolls, bracketing, trying other angles, etc. This is good, because it gives the customer a large selection of photographs to choose from. However, the photographer retains ownership of any photographs not chosen, and these can be sold to other clients.

The best bet is to get a signed stipulation that you are paying for the photographer's services, but that you retain all negatives, prints, slides, etc., *and outtakes.* The next best bet is to negotiate for the initial use and to set a fee for any subsequent use.

SUMMARY AND CONCLUSION

PERSONAL PHOTOGRAPHY

Ads by the manufacturers of cameras and film have made us think that good photography "just happens" when we aim at our subject and shoot. That we believe such things is unfortunate for professional photographers and for us, too, because it means that we have so few really good portraits of family and friends to help us think of them while they are with us and to remember them when they are gone. A professional photographer, on the other hand, will not only provide us with a photo of higher technical quality, but one that is more aesthetically pleasing as well, for a good photographer, like a good painter, manages to capture the inner person as well as the externals.

Professional photographs will never replace home-made candids or "snapshots." Hopefully, in addition to visiting a regular photographer, you will continue taking those. You'll find your home photos improving, incidentally, if you read some good books on photography, if you take five or six shots of a scene instead of one, and if you bracket half-stop over and half-stop under for protection.

COMMERCIAL PHOTOGRAPHY

As a former co-owner of the first exclusive multimedia production company in Texas and a writer of sales, safety, and training programs for business and industry, I've worked with $500-a-day photographers and with $2,000-a-day photographers. Is there a difference? Usually. In a free enterprise system, prices are set by demand, and everyone tends to charge as much as he can get, as long as it's not more than he's worth. While you might find a genius that does not yet know it and is, therefore, under-priced, the odds are against it.

Buying photography is like buying carpet or anything else. What do you need? Most of the time, you need clear, sharp, dramatic shots. For those, a middle-priced photographer can fit the bill nicely. If you're wanting awards or you're trying to create a mood, an atmosphere, an image, or an ethereal feeling, then you need something more.

Following these tips and tactics should help you get what you need at a price you're willing to pay.

Plumber

OVERVIEW

The word *plumber* comes from the Latin *plumbum*, meaning "lead," because lead pipes once carried water to the homes of rich Romans. At the time, lead seemed perfect for the task—it is soft, malleable, and has a low melting point. Then, too, Roman aristocrats also felt that lead added to the flavor of their wine, and liked to pour wine from lead pitchers into their goblets. What they didn't realize, however, was that lead leached out of pipe and pitcher, causing a condition called *plumbism*, or "lead poisoning"! Symptoms include headache, nausea, mood swings, irritability, and irrational behavior. Some put part of the blame for the decadence of the latter emperors and the decline of the empire on *lead poisoning among the leading politicians and generals.*

In these enlightened times, we know about lead poisoning and we use PVC or copper pipes for our water. However, some older homes might have some lead contamination from the solder once used to join copper pipe. That's why, if you have an older home, it's a good idea to let the tap run a minute before drinking the water in order to allow any lead to pass out of the pipe.

Plumbers, admittedly unwittingly, helped bring down the

Roman Empire. Today, using modern methods and tools, plumbers keep our water and sewage systems working while making certain that "never the twain shall meet." They are also taught antisiphoning techniques, so they can prevent stagnated water from entering our drinking water. They are pretty important persons in our civilization, and it is important that they be highly trained and knowledgeable.

I have upon occasion proven myself very adept at solving electrical problems. I can even put in a circuit alone and unaided. Plumbing, however, is quite another matter, and I will admit that most of it is beyond me. I can't keep a garden hose from leaking. I'll never forget the time I decided to stop a leak underneath the kitchen sink. It was then that I discovered "slip joints," those insidious little things that allow the traps or "j-bends" coming from a double sink, a garbage disposal, and a dishwasher to all exit into a common pipe. As soon as I got one not to leak, its neighbor began leaking, and so on, almost as if the various plumbing components found it terribly amusing. After a couple of hours of water torture, I decided two things: One, I would never meet the person who designed slip joints in heaven, as there must surely be some sins that cannot be atoned for. Two, I was going to call a plumber.

If you're like me, and all thumbs when it comes to plumbing, then you need to know a good plumber. They are *not* all equal. I've had one tell me that vile-smelling slime oozing from a septic tank was normal, try to collect his fee for a service call, and go on. Another time, a plumber came out to check a leak of clean, clear water that began to accumulate around the base of a toilet seat. He told my wife it was probably backing up from the septic tank, to call a septic repairman—and handed her a bill for a service call. When I told him I *knew* what water backing up from the septic tank looked like, his boss came out, examined the toilet seat, and told my wife it must have an "invisible crack" in it and would have to be replaced. She pointed out an area that had once been caulked, but the caulking was gone, and suggested he try that. Reluctantly, he did—and the leak was history.

I suppose the bottom line is that while all plumbers are better trained than me, some must either have momentary relapses or not be quite honest. Here's how to find a well-trained, smart, honest plumber of your own!

TIPS AND TACTICS

1. Get a recommendation.

Ask your friends and neighbors, or, if you're new in an area, call a couple of churches or restaurants and ask who they use. Take down the name and ask if their plumber:

- is prompt
- does good work
- cleans up after himself
- gives reasonable estimates
- gives invoices that match the estimates

2. Know what it takes to be a good plumber.

In Texas, plumbers are licensed. You need a *journeyman's* license to be a plumber and a *master's* license to own a plumbing business. A *journeyman's* certificate means the plumber has spent at least eight thousand hours of apprenticeship and study, and passed a four-hour written and a four-hour practical test. If his certificate is new, then it means he's passed a test that takes twice that long! That's just the beginning, because to keep his license, a plumber must have six hours of continuing education each year!

When you call *any* licensed plumber in Texas, you should get a journeyman or master plumber. Apprentices, who are also licensed, are not allowed to work unsupervised, and will always be under the direct supervision of a licensed plumber. Therefore, in my home state, you are pretty well protected when it comes to experience, and can concentrate on finding a plumber who is also honest and hardworking.

To find out what the requirements are in your state, call the local plumbing board or any licensed plumber in the Yellow Pages. If your state has a tough standard, you can feel comfortable about the *knowledge* the plumber has. If your state has a lax standard, then you're going to have to move on to tip number three.

3. Ask your plumber how much experience he has.

The amount of experience and knowledge your state requires is the *minimum*. The more experience and knowledge your plumber has, the less time it will take to sort out and repair your problems. Always go with a plumber that's been around long enough that he can look at a problem and think, Hey, I've done that before. I know just what to do!

4. Ask if they're bonded and insured.

The bond covers the honesty of their employees, the insurance covers any damage they might do. (More than one fire has been caused by a plumber's torch.)

5. Ask how they bill.

Some plumbers charge by the hour. Others will give you a flat fee. Personally, all other things being equal, I'll always take the known over the unknown. On big jobs, it makes sense to get bids from more than one plumber, unless you feel very comfortable with the plumber and the price. On small jobs, remember that most plumbers charge by the hour with a one-hour minimum, so if you have any other small plumbing jobs that need to be done while he's there, be sure to ask him to do those, too.

6. Always be ready to stop the project.

There's nothing wrong with getting an estimate, thanking the plumber, saying, "I'll get back to you," and hanging up. Also, if you get an uneasy feeling once the plumber is there, you can always call a halt to the proceedings and say, "I'd like to get a second opinion."

SUMMARY AND CONCLUSION

The state of Texas, which doesn't license electricians, somehow managed to get very, very stringent regulations in place to help protect its citizens from hack plumbers. Beware of those "plumbers" who are not actually plumbers. A lot of people who run "handyman" ads will offer to do plumbing, but they might or might not be trained and/or licensed to do it!

A plumber licensed in this state knows plumbing and knows the way things ought to be. Yet, codes vary from place to place. When I lived in Wood County, if you were outside the city limits, there were no standards for electricity, sewer, or plumbing systems. Therefore, a builder could, and did, put in whatever seemed right in his own eyes. Here in Williamson County, *all* houses, rural as well as urban, must be built to national codes. That's what you want where you are: qualified people doing work to a known standard. The standards are there for a reason—don't acquiesce to shortcuts.

But we have a right to expect more than competence. We have a right to expect *service*. The plumber you choose should provide fast, friendly, reasonably priced service. He should do what he says he'll do, when he says he'll do it, and for the price he says he'll charge. And you shouldn't have to shampoo carpets or mop floors to clean up his mess afterward. When your plumber leaves, he should leave your place like he found it—only with the plumbing problem fixed. With a little preplanning and a little effort, you can find a plumber who will do just that!

Printer

Until Johann Gutenberg developed movable type in 1450, all books were hand drawn and handwritten. Consequently, you had to be a very wealthy and important person to hold a book like this in your hands. Gutenberg's method, setting a book one wooden letter at a time, took a lot more time than copying one by hand. However, once Gutenberg had the book set, he could run off dozens, hundreds, thousands, or tens of thousands of copies.

In Shakespeare's time, nobody worried about spelling, because they felt if the reader could figure it out, it didn't matter. In the early days of printing, no one worried if the print was sharp and clear, figuring that as long as you could read it, it didn't matter. Today, however, we're no longer willing to overlook sloppy spelling or printing.

In the nearly nineteen years in which I've been "self-unemployed," I have had much experience with printers. In the early years, I often experienced disappointment over inept attempts to reproduce my reversed logo. (*Reversed* means that instead of the logo being in color, the area around the logo is in color, and the logo is simply the color of the paper stock. In my particular case, the logo is on white paper stock, and the bar around it is in blue. Here's how it looks in black and white:

A good printer has no problem with my logo. Poor printers seem to have trouble getting the blue bar properly inked, especially on envelopes. Poor printers always seem to blame the blotching on the seam in the envelope. Good printers, using envelopes of the same brand and weight, don't seem to have that problem. Consequently, I have learned to shun poor printers.

An artist friend of mine, Larry Daste, designed the logo for me when I sold my first magazine article back in 1972. Anyway, it's a wonderful logo, and over the years I've had many, many compliments on it. Some say it fits my character. I assume they mean my character matches the character of the knight charging windmills, not the horse carrying him!

Larry designed the logo straight. That is, he drew in Don Quixote, and the horse, and the pen, and the windmill, and suggested that I tell the printer to reverse it in a blue bar with the edge of the illustrations bleeding open. I did. He did. The result was a great print job. However, when I asked the printer for my original back, he said, "You'd better let us keep that for you, because we have a place to store it, and you probably don't." That sounded good to me, so I left it.

Six months later, I went back to get more letterhead printed. "Do you have your original artwork?" he asked. "No, you're keeping it," I replied. He shook his head, "No, you must be mistaken. We never keep clients' art. Hell, if we did, we'd need a warehouse just to store all of it!"

Long ago, I learned that you can't get very far arguing with a man that'll look you square in the eye and tell you a lie without even blinking. Therefore, I didn't so much as cry "Liar! Liar! Pants on fire!" as I exited the building. I did, however, punish him in the most effective way possible: I took my business elsewhere and advised any friends looking for a good printer to do likewise.

Besides learning to retain my own print elements, I've also learned how to find a good printer. Some of my tips, along with some from the pros, are listed below.

TIPS AND TACTICS

1. Call someone whose brochure or letterhead you admire and ask for recommendations.
Most businesses will be happy to tell you who does their printing.

2. Check the Yellow Pages.
The ads can be quite informative. Look for someone who has been in business for several years.

3. Visit some prospects.
Explain exactly what you want. For instance, when I'm having letterhead done, I show a sample and say, "This is the kind of stock and the kind of print job that I want. Nothing less than this will be acceptable. For example, I

notice that some printers have a problem with the blue bar, particularly on envelopes. I will expect the blue bar to be evenly inked and the type to be clear and sharp. Can you do a job to this standard?"

My method might sound a bit harsh, but there is no need in wasting their time and my money if they can't do the work. Surprisingly, even though letterhead is one of the simplest things to print, I've had printers tell me that they couldn't reach my quality standards.

While you're visiting the prospect, ask to see samples of his work. *Ask if all the printing is done in-house or if some of it is sent out.* (There is no need for you to pay a double markup if he isn't doing the work anyway.) If you need a brochure or color work, ask what the color charge is, if they have a graphic arts department, and about turnaround.[32] Also ask, "Do you have the right equipment to do this job? Is the equipment you have the *best choice* for this kind of job?" Sure, a printer *could* fib to you, but when he's definitely told you they can do the work, and that he has the right equipment for the job, you are in very good position to complain should something go wrong.

4. Ask for referrals.

As I have said over and over in this book, referrals are worthless unless you call and check them. Sometimes, you'll be surprised to find what some of the customers

....

[32] A word of caution: Never make expensive plans based on an unproved printer's promise that the work will be ready on a certain day! Trust me, you have a big chance of regretting it if you trust him to deliver on time and you don't have a "fallback" position!

they used as a reference *really* thought about a print job. Most people are too nice to complain. They just decide, "Well, next time, I'll go somewhere else!" Yet, when you call and ask them if they'd recommend the person who gave you their name, they'll tell you no and tell you why. What is really sad is if the customer had told the printer the reason he was unhappy, the printer would have had an opportunity to make it right and could have not only had that customer happy, but you as a happy customer, too! That's why I always advise people to complain if they're unhappy. They can't get any unhappier—and they just might get happy!

SUMMARY AND CONCLUSION

In this section, I've concentrated on the type of printing most people need most often: letterhead, envelopes, business cards, flyers, etc. If you need more complex work, involving multiple colors or full color, binding, computer graphics, etc., and the printer you selected for your routine work cannot help you, they, being professionals, will refer you to someone who can.

Frankly, for routine items such as those described above, I've found very little difference in the cost of printing when I priced small places and large firms. Naturally, you'll pay more for a high-quality print job than you will a low-quality one, but if you'll order in larger quantities, you can usually offset much of the difference. The biggest expense in doing letterhead, envelopes, or brochures, is set-up time. Once the press is running, you'll pay more to do two thousand copies than you would five hundred—but not *four times as much.* That's because, while you do have four times as much paper, you do not have four times as much labor. Modern presses practically run themselves.

Note: No matter what they tell you, take your original artwork home with you when the job is completed.

Real Estate Agent

Will Rogers said, "I never met a man I didn't like." Although I've since changed my mind, there was a time in my life when I figured old Will must have never met a real estate agent. I've met agents who were rude, pushy, and obstinate. Real estate agents who didn't listen to what I wanted to *buy*, merely wanted me to listen to what they wanted to *sell*. And I've had some who, upon hearing I was going to sell my own home, were downright rude. Fortunately, I've lived long enough to buy several houses and parcels of real estate, and I have met some really superlative real estate agents, too. I want to help you get one of the great ones.

One of the things I've learned from the bad real estate agents was that I didn't have to have a real estate agent at all to sell my own property. I once worked in sales, I've written sales seminars, and I coauthored a book on selling. Therefore, I sold my last two houses myself. I had a sign painted, I had data sheets prepared, I ran advertising, and I showed the home at *my convenience*. If you have selling skills, you can do the same. True, there is some legal paperwork to do to settle your mortgage, transfer ownership and all of that, but you're paying a title company to do that whether or not you use a real estate agent. When it came time to close, there was just one less person present than when a real estate agent handled the transaction.

I sold my first home because the first real estate agent I contacted was arrogant, conceited, and condescending. In addition, he said something that I felt was unrealistic. He smiled and said, "My fee won't cost *you* anything, because we'll just tack it on to what you want to get for the house!" I figured the only way I could get away with tacking the fee onto the price I wanted for the house would be if it were a seller's market (it wasn't) or if the buyer parachuted in from Mars with a suitcase full of money and had no knowledge of what property was worth. Otherwise, *somewhere* in the process of buying a home, a *professional appraiser* would come out and tell them what the home was *really* worth. *That* figure wouldn't be the fair market value plus the real estate agent's 6 percent[33] commission, it would be the fair market value *alone.* And even if it did include the fair market value with the real estate agent's commission figured in, if I didn't pay it to him, it would be left there for me.

Yet, if you lack selling expertise, and/or marketing expertise, and/or time, a real estate agent can handle *much* (not "all," or "most," but "much!") of the hassle for you

....

[33] I've checked both the Ten Commandments and the Constitution of the United States, along with the amendments to the latter. Nowhere does it state that a real estate agent *must* be paid a 6 percent commission. It is more or less standard, but like everything else in real estate, it *is* negotiable.

and can probably move the property faster. But, there's no free lunch. Your real estate agent might be the nicest person you ever meet, but he's in that business to make money and he's going to make money selling your house, even if you don't! If you're buying a home, don't feel you're off the hook, because the seller and the seller's real estate agent will be working as hard as they can to see that *you* cover part of that fee.

Okay, what do we have here? We have the buyer and his real estate agent looking out for him. Who is looking out for you? Well, if you drive by and see the sign and call his real estate agent, in most states, the only guy on your team is you. There are exceptions. If you go to another real estate firm and ask them to show you that house, they'll be splitting the commission with the listing real estate agent, but your real estate agent will be looking out for you, because the only way he has a chance to make a cent is if you buy the house. However, in some states, such as Texas, you have a choice of who the agent represents, and you can insist upon an agent who represents your interests being part of the transaction.

LISTING AGREEMENTS

If you're a seller, the real estate agent will try to get you to sign a listing agreement giving them exclusive rights to sell your house for a specified period of time. If you sign such an agreement, take the shortest period you can, because if an agent has more properties than prospects, the natural tendency will be to try to move the listings he's about to lose *first*. If they have you on the hook for a year, you might have to wait awhile before they get really, really serious about moving your property. Besides, a shorter-term agreement can always be extended, and should you find you're roosting with turkeys instead of soaring with eagles, you can correct the matter much sooner. For the life of the contract, however, the real estate agent with the listing will collect the agreed-on percentage *regardless* of who sells the house. If a competing real estate agent sells it, they'll split the commission. If *you* find a prospect at work and sell the house, the real estate agent will collect the full commission.

You do not have to sign a listing agreement. Sometimes real estate agents prospect by calling those who have signs reading, "For Sale by Owner" and say, "I've got a prospect for your house. If you'll sign with me, I'll bring him out." To that, I've always responded, "Great, I'll sign an agreement for that one client, and if he buys, I'll pay you __ percent." If the real estate agent agrees, he probably *really* has a client, and if you like the way he handles himself, you might want to do a formal listing agreement.

If you're a buyer, some real estate agents will try to sign you to an exclusive contract, too, explaining that without a signed agreement, the seller is represented. If I were to sign one, it would be on a particular piece of property, not carte blanche. Naturally, as long as the agent is listening and working for me, I want to stay with him, but I won't eliminate all other options. Let me tell you a couple of true stories to illustrate what I mean!

STORY NO. 1:

The Rotten Real Estate Agent

As a freelance writer, I bill for my time. On days when I don't work as a writer, quite naturally, I don't get paid. Therefore, when I was looking for a new home in the fall of 1980, I wanted to be certain the real estate agent understood exactly what we were looking for before I made the commitment to take a day off and make a two-hundred-mile round-trip to look at houses. I told her, "I want a house of about twenty-five hundred square feet, with either four bedrooms or three bedrooms and an office. It must be in an area served by my current telephone company, there must be at least three-quarters of an acre of ground, and the house cannot need any painting." (See "How to Find an Expert: Painter.")

When she called, told me that she had several houses lined up, and asked me to come down; we did. In four hours, we saw several interesting houses, yet, not a single one had twenty-five hundred square feet. Not a single one had four bedrooms or three bedrooms and an office. Not a single one was in the service area of the right telephone company. Every single one needed painting. Not a single one was on at least three-quarters of an acre.

When I complained, the real estate agent replied, "Well, maybe you'll like this next one!" The next one was an 1,800-square-foot house, had the wrong telephone company, was on a quarter-acre lot, needed painting, and had just three bedrooms with no office. When I pointed this out, the real estate agent smiled and said,

"But wait!" Then, she triumphantly led me outside, and with a flourish, showed me an old-fashioned, glassed-in greenhouse measuring about twelve-by-eighteen. She opened the door and held it for me to step inside. As my feet crunched on the gravel floor, I turned and said, "So? I don't want a greenhouse!"

She smiled and said, "Yes, but I'm sure *with your imagination, you can see what a great office this would make for a writer*!" I laughed and replied, "One of my clients is an electric company. They'd have to put in a substation to generate enough power for me to air-condition a greenhouse, and when I turned the power off on the weekend, my computer would melt!"

Why did she waste my time? A couple of reasons. First, bringing us into all those homes persuaded the home owners that she was really working hard, bringing in prospects. Second, she hoped that we'd see something we liked so much that we'd forget it didn't meet any of our criteria. As a result, she wasted my time, her time, and the time of every home owner we visited. She also lost me as a prospect.

After this bad trip, I called another real estate agent and gave her the same instructions. She found a house that met our criteria and we bought it. Then the first real estate agent called me at home and chewed me out for being disloyal! I patiently explained that:

1. Lincoln freed the slaves, so no human being could own another.

2. Since she could not show me a single house that met

any of my criteria, I quite naturally went to someone who could.

The only thing that made my expensive and exasperating relationship with that real estate agent bearable was *that it lasted just a single day*! Think how miserable I would have been had I *signed an exclusive contract that I wouldn't buy a house in that community within a specified period of time unless I bought it through her*!

STORY NO. 2.
The Right Real Estate Agent

When we moved to Georgetown, I got referrals to a real estate company, checked them out, and selected an agent. Remembering my problems a dozen years before, I handed her a typewritten list of what I wanted:

- a brick or stone house of at least twenty-eight hundred square feet
- at least a one-acre lot if the house for sale and/or the houses in the neighborhood were single-story, and at least two acres if that house or any in the neighborhood were two stories
- no front-entry garage
- a nice, quiet neighborhood
- lots of windows
- a large living room
- a large den
- built-ins in the kitchen
- no skylights
- a sprinkler system

- a house that didn't need paint!

When we came into town to look at homes, she said, "Well, your requirements were very specific, so I don't have a *lot* of homes to show you, but every one I do have meets all your criteria." She spoke the gospel truth, and we bought one of the homes we toured that day.

Now, how *could you like* a real estate agent like the first one I told you about? How could you *not like* a real estate agent like the second one I mentioned? That second real estate agent listened. She researched. She only showed me houses that met my criteria, and she sold me a house. No hassle. *No wasted effort by anyone.*

All I want for you is a real estate agent like the one just described. Here's how you get one.

BUYER TIPS AND TACTICS

1. Decide what you want.

Write down just what you want in a house, including a price range. The more specific you are, the more difficult it will be for them to locate you a house, but the less likely you are to waste a lot of time looking at homes that don't meet your criteria. (If you're one of those folks who likes surprises and frequently remark, "I would never have believed I'd have liked such and such, but when she showed it to me, I just fell in love with it!," then you probably shouldn't make your list too comprehensive. Not even the best real estate agent is a mind reader.)

2. Ask around.

If you are moving from one city to another, ask a real

estate agent you trust to find you someone just as good at your new location. (He will share the commission on the sale, so your current real estate agent will have a vested interest in taking care of you!) Another good strategy is to ask someone whose opinion you respect in the town where you're moving. Also, just driving around and checking the signs will give you a good idea of who the movers and shakers are. Also, check the local newspaper for ads. Good real estate agents don't just wait for someone to drive by and see their signs, they aggressively market their properties.

3. Select your real estate agent.

It must be clearly understood by everyone concerned that *your* real estate agent represents *you* and not the *seller*. Once that occurs, your agent becomes your partner in helping you find a home. Therefore, you want someone who is competent, considerate, capable, and congenial, because otherwise, he will begin to rub you the wrong way fast. In addition, you want a real estate agent who:

- is a member of MLS (multiple listing service). (This means he can show properties offered by other real estate agents, so you'll have access to more buyers. Understand, however, that each real estate agent will try to sell his own properties first if he can, because then they don't have to split the commission.)
- maintains, either in hard copy or on slides or computer, a data sheet on all his properties, showing interior and exterior photos, amenities, dimensions, etc.

(This will save you a lot of time in that you can immediately reject a house that you wouldn't care to see.)

■ has a large number of listings in your price range or is willing to "cut to the chase" and show you other listings right off the bat

■ who listens and only shows you houses that obviously meet *most* of your criteria

■ treats you with respect, as an individual

■ tells you what he *really* thinks a house is worth or can be purchased for

4. Level with your real estate agent.

As a general rule of thumb, you can qualify for a loan so long as you have a good credit history and your PITI (principle, interest, taxes, and insurance) doesn't exceed 28 to 38 percent of your income. (The spread depends on your other debt.) You keep the PITI within range by increasing the size of your down payment. If, however, you have champagne tastes and a beer budget, your real estate agent isn't going to be able to make the numbers work, no matter how hard he tries. Therefore, if you have credit problems, if your down payment will be small, if you have a lot of short-term consumer debt, *level with your real estate agent*. He can only help you if you are honest.

5. Leave your real estate agent if he doesn't perform.

If the real estate agent can't find you the kind of house you're looking for, it's time to move on. Here are some other reasons to change real estate agents:

- if he doesn't have data sheets to show you before you visit a house
- if he doesn't return your calls
- if he betrays a confidence, such as making the opening gambit with your "final offer"
- if he is pushy instead of pleasant
- if he acts like the fact you haven't found a house is your fault because you're hard to please
- if he forgets that Lincoln freed the slaves and acts like he owns you, forgetting that you have the freedom to shop elsewhere

SELLER TIPS AND TACTICS

Your real estate agent is going to be your senior partner in selling your home. Therefore, you want someone who is competent, considerate, capable, and congenial, because otherwise, he or she will begin to rub you the wrong way fast. Pay special attention to these tips and tactics.

1. Decide what you want for your home.

If it were my house, I'd call a couple of mortgage companies and ask them to recommend some appraisers. Then, I'd get a professional appraisal, not merely a comparative marketing analysis, *before* I called a real estate agent. I'd decide what my absolute bottom line was, including real estate agent fees, closing costs, etc. I would not reveal this number to anyone, even under torture.

2. Select your real estate agent.

Your real estate agent is going to be your partner in selling your home, so you need to have a nice "fit." You don't have to become best friends, but you should develop a high level of communication and trust. In addition, you want a real estate agent who:

■ is a member of MLS (This means other real estate agents can also show your home. Naturally, all real estate agents prefer to sell their own listings because then they don't have to split commissions. But if they can't meet a prospect's needs with their own properties, they'll show listings held by other real estate agents.)

■ maintains, either in hard copy or on slides or computer, a data sheet on all their properties, showing interior and exterior photos, amenities, dimensions, etc. (This will save you a lot of time in that buyers won't be coming through your home unless they show a preliminary interest.)

■ will tell you what they think the house is really worth (Some unscrupulous folks will say almost anything in order to get a listing and suggest you take almost anything to make the sale. After all, if you come down ten thousand dollars, they lose just six hundred dollars in commissions—you lose ten thousand dollars. They won't pay for a professional appraisal, of course, but they can probably give you a CMA [comparative marketing analysis] that shows what other houses in the area have sold for. However, since a CMA does not take into consideration individual differences, this is only a guideline.)

will advertise your property in the newspaper, put up signs, arrange open houses, etc.

will only show your home to valid prospects

3. ***How to know when you've chosen the wrong real estate agent.***

Despite your best efforts, it is possible that your real estate agent is just a turkey in an eagle suit. Should this happen, you will be very glad that you signed a *short* contract. Wait it out and try again elsewhere. Signs that you picked a turkey are:

He promised he could get you far more than your appraisal or the CMA.

He says, "My fee won't cost you anything!" and then brings you a bunch of bids which are well below that figure or even below the professional appraisal you had done. (You did have the professional appraisal done, didn't you?)

He didn't perform as promised; i.e., he didn't run ads, arrange an open house, etc.

He doesn't return your telephone calls.

He didn't create a data sheet on your house, complete with amenities, photos, etc.

SUMMARY AND CONCLUSION

Buying or selling a house is an ordeal, whether you do it yourself or engage a real estate agent to help you. A really good real estate agent can save you a lot of time and hassle, and will bring in a wider array of houses (if you're a buyer) or prospects (if you're a seller) than you'd have otherwise. The good real estate agent is a nice, caring person. Like the rest of us, however, he isn't in business just to be a nice, caring person. He is in business to make money. Therefore, do not think that the real estate agent is going to do all of this for free. If you're a shrewd buyer, and only pay what a house appraises for, the real estate agent fees will all come out of the seller's pocket. In that case, the seller's compensation will be that he sold the house with less hassle and time than it would have taken had he done it himself. If you're a shrewd seller, you'll see to it that your real estate agent gets you enough in the transaction to recoup *some* of your selling expenses.

As we prepare to go to press, I feel that I must add a final warning. Take nothing in real estate on trust, but get everything in writing. If you're buying a home, get an outside inspector to give you a written report. Do not depend on the honesty of the seller, nor upon the fact that your agent, having been party to the conversation, will speak up and admit it later. Trust me, I know what I'm talking about. Besides, I put it in writing.

Remodeler

Remodeling is one of those words that means different things to different people. Therefore, in the Yellow Pages, you'll find everyone from bathtub, to tile, to cabinet re-finishers to builders and cabinetmakers listed in the re-modeling section. In this segment, we shall deal with remodelers who are actually going to be *building* some-thing, such as adding additional space to a structure, i.e., a room addition or patio, or those who are renovating an existing structure, such as replacing kitchen cabinets and counters, turning two rooms into one, one into two, etc.

Before beginning, however, I'd like to give you a one-question quiz.

Q. If you are remodeling, and you pay the contractor, but he does not pay all his suppliers, who is liable?

A. If you are like most people, you replied, "the contractor." If so, you were wrong—*you are responsible*! [34]

I can hear you saying what I said when I first heard this: "Hey, wait a minute; that's not fair!"

[34] In all fairness, remodelers have told me that there have been times when, *after paying all their suppliers and subcontractors*, they weren't paid by the home owner! So it behooves both of you to be a bit cautious and to make certain your agreement is in writing!

So, who said life was fair? Fair or not, that is the way the world works. That's why our lending sources tell us that building is more fraught with risk than any other area of real estate. It doesn't happen often, because most businesses are in business to stay in business and are honest—but it *does happen.* Therefore, if you are considering remodeling, I strongly urge you to begin by turning back and reading the section under "How to Find An Expert: Building Contractor." Once you have done that, proceed to the tips and tactics below.

TIPS AND TACTICS

1. Decide exactly what you want to do.

Take your "before" photos, and get multiple prints made. Then mark the prints "A," "B," "C," etc. Next, write down exactly what you want done in each area shown in the photographs. When you feel that your photos and instructions are crystal clear, show them to a friend or neighbor who knows nothing about your project. Without any coaching, have them read your written list and look at the photos. Then question them about what *they think* you want done. When you get your instructions so clear that a nonprofessional can understand them, you are ready to talk to a remodeler.

You can now show each remodeler you visit *exactly what you want and where you want it.* This will help them bid materials and manpower more accurately and will provide each of you with a written record of what was asked for and what was agreed to.

If you are wanting to remodel and you have only a vague overview of what you want, then you're going to need a remodeler who can work with you to help you design your project. If this is the case, the remodeler deserves to be compensated for that design time should you select someone else, and you should discuss this going into the negotiations.

2. Get recommendations.

Remembering the pitfalls in construction work, never use any remodeler who wasn't recommended by someone you trust. There are several places you can go for trustworthy recommendations:

- Ask friends. When you ask friends, don't just ask, "Have you heard of anyone who is good?" Ask, "Is there anyone you have used who you would recommend?" If they say another friend used that person and the work was good, call that friend and check out the story before proceeding.

- Ask your banker or mortgage lender who they would recommend if they were financing the project.

- Go to the hall of records and pull up remodeling building permits. Note the names, call those who had the work done, ask how the job went, and if they were satisfied.

- Run your final list past the local building inspector. He has seen everyone's work and will have firsthand knowledge of who is competent and who is not.

- Call the Better Business Bureau and run your short list of candidates past them.

3. *Call some remodelers and invite them to talk with you at their place.*

True, he will have to come to your place eventually, but it's nice to see that your remodeler has a place of business, not just a set of wheels and a mobile phone. If you took photos, show them and the written description of what you want done. If you didn't take photos, hand them the written description. Then you need to ask:

- ■ Does this sound like a job you are qualified to do?
- ■ Do you have experience doing jobs like this?
- ■ How long have you been in business in this area?[35]
- ■ What would you charge to do the job, including any sketches that we might need? (He will tell you, truthfully, that he will have to come out and see the site, but asking now sets up the next question.)
- ■ Do your own crews do all of the work, or is some of it subcontracted? If some is subcontracted, how do you guarantee quality? How will I know that you've paid all your subs? (If he doesn't have a good payment verification system, before you make your last payment, require him to sign a notarized statement that says, "I have paid all my suppliers and subcontractors, and nothing is owed to anyone on this project." Refer to the section under "How to Find an Expert: Building Contractor" for more details.)

....

[35] If you are told that he is new to this area, but worked for a number of years in another area, find out the company name he was using there and check references at the previous location. People move for a lot of very good reasons. On rare occasions, a poor reputation is one of them.

4. *Go out and look at some of the remodeler's jobs.*

It is probable that he will be more than willing to call some former customers and get permission to bring you out and see what was done. You should also call a couple of his other references and check them out.

5. *Check the financial details.*

Minor jobs should be paid for only upon completion. If, for instance, the contractor doesn't have the finances to cover the materials for a deck, then he really isn't in business. He's just a carpenter looking for work. If I *had* to pay for the materials in advance, I'd get a complete list of what was needed, check competitive prices, pay for it myself, and have it delivered, making sure that materials came off the remodeler's written estimate.

This sounds very distrustful. Actually, I'm a very trustful person. It's just that, like former Vice President Dan Quayle said about politics, "The hardest thing for me to accept was that someone could look you in the eye and lie, because I wasn't raised that way." *One time*, I allowed a contractor to get a check for materials instead of arranging for the delivery myself. That was the last I saw of the contractor or the money. I'm still a trusting guy, except now, I'm a bit more cautious. I'd like to save you the eight hundred dollars that lesson cost me!

Trust, however, is a two-way street, and many honest remodelers have had trouble collecting all their money after a job. So don't be surprised if the contractor asks you for financial data or wants you to sign a contract. Asking doesn't mean that he doesn't trust you, just that, like you, he wants to be protected in case the kind of thing that "hardly ever happens" happens!

6. Get bids.

Always get at least two, preferably three bids. As you get bids, however, be certain that you compare quality of materials and workmanship. If your project requires only basic skills and simple materials, then cost will be very important to you. If, however, you are looking for quality materials and quality workmanship, you won't want to spend more than you must, but you will realize that quality always costs more initially.

SUMMARY AND CONCLUSION

Tim Todd, one of the remodelers we interviewed, said, "Something that home owners almost never consider when contemplating a remodeling project, especially a major remodeling project, is the impact on their privacy and lifestyle. Sure, they know it's going to be inconvenient at times, and messy, but they don't realize how inconvenient it is really going to be. Home owners will sometimes suffer from 'remodel burnout' toward the end of the job and relations can become strained between spouses, and between home owners and the contractor. It's important that communications remain open."

Mr. Todd went on to say that unexpected problems and/or owner-directed changes can increase the time to do the job and also add to the cost, so have some contingency funds set aside just in case, and always arrive at a bottom-line cost before any changes are made. In other words, if you get halfway through the job and you have a brainstorm, be sure you get a firm idea of how much that will add to the cost before you stop your remodeler and send him off in a new direction!

The sages say, "When it comes to quality, you get what you pay for." Well, you do if you're careful. Carpenters have a saying: "Measure *once*, cut *twice*. Measure *twice*, cut once." They're saying that if you take the time to make certain you're right before you go ahead, things will turn out right on the first pass. If you get in a hurry, well, then you get into trouble. Take plenty of time to think through exactly what you want done. Take plenty of time to pick the right remodeler to do it for you. Then, the odds are in your favor that your job will be completed on time, on target, and on budget.

Résumé Service

In the old days, when the economy went into a downturn, businesses and manufacturers had "layoffs." As high taxes at home and low wages abroad began moving manufacturing jobs out of the country, more and more businesses began having "layoffs." We reacted to increasing doses of bad news by changing the nomenclature, and "layoff" became politically incorrect. So instead of saying "layoff," we said, "cutback." "Cutbacks," in time, fell to the term "downsizing," which has become, in these more politically enlightened times, "right sizing."

Whatever word they used when they gave you the bad news, it meant that you needed to find another job. When this happened to a friend of mine at a major manufacturing company, I called and said, "Hey, if you need help with a résumé or marketing yourself, give me a call. I'll give you a 100 percent discount off my usual exorbitant rate."

He replied, "Marc, I appreciate it, but they're giving us a class on how to write a résumé as part of our separation package. Don't you think that would be enough?" I said, "Sure, if you want your résumé to look like all the others in the class!"

Anyone can pick up a book at the library, and copy the format and come up with a résumé that looks just like everyone else's. But if you want to stand apart from the rest who are chasing the same job, you will want to showcase what makes you special and differentiates you from the competition. A good résumé service can help pull you from the pack and put you on the inside track for employment again.

Understand, however, that a résumé service is not a job placement service. Their task is not to get you a job. Their task is to get you a résumé that will help you get the job you want.

TIPS AND TACTICS

1. Ask around.

Ask people who've just been hired who did their résumés. Call personnel managers at companies in your area, and say, "It's been several years since I've done a résumé. Since I know you see a lot of them, I thought you might be able to recommend a good résumé service." (That is also a good way to meet some personnel managers! One might well ask, "Well, what kind of job are you looking for? What have you done before?" All that could lead to a job interview at a company whose "right size" just might include you!) Also ask at your local library to see if there is a local job-hunting resource center. (Many libraries now offer this as a free service!)

2. Do a self-assessment.

You've lost your job, and it is natural to feel rejection and self-doubt. This will pass. Chances are, it wasn't your fault. If it was, well, you can learn from the experience and keep it from happening again. Either way, you can emerge from this a better employee and a better person. Make a list of your likes and dislikes, your strong points and your weak ones. Begin thinking about careers where your long suits will hold you in good stead and make you a valuable employee. Chances are, you've a lot more going for you than you thought!

3. Decide what you want.

Do you want just a résumé, or would you like a cover letter, too? The better services use laser printers, and they can not only provide you with typeset résumés but can create "letterhead" so you can send each prospect a personal cover letter.

4. Call some résumé services or résumé writers.

If you know what you want, they should be able to give you a price range over the telephone. I say "price range" because if everything was done for a "flat fee," I'd think that maybe I was talking to a *typist* instead of a *writer*. A *typist* takes what you have written and makes it look pretty. A *writer* takes what you have written, adds what he learns about you in the interview, and makes it look *exciting.* Give special credence to a résumé service or résumé writer who:

- has experience writing résumés for people in your profession
- asks you to come in for a personal consultation (A good résumé will not only convey your credentials, but something of your personality.)
- has been in the business for several years

- can show you samples of his work
- stores your résumé in word processing so that extra copies or updates are simple, easy, and inexpensive
- offers mailing or fax service
- has worked in business or industry interviewing prospective employees and has seen both good and bad résumés and knows which is which and why!
- can give job-search advice or tell you where to go for that information
- can give you interviewing tips or tell you where to go for that information

5. *Try it his way first.*

Okay, you've found a person who meets all your qualifications, and you feel comfortable with him. But you're not certain that you should follow his instructions. What do you do? If it were me, I'd give it a chance. After all, we go to a résumé service for the same reason we go to a doctor: We have a problem and don't know what to do about it. Why not at least *try* the doctor's medicine?

SUMMARY AND CONCLUSION

There was a long period of time in America when a person went to work for a company and stayed there until he retired. People were proud of their ten-year service pins and twenty-year service pins. Then things began to change. Competition put companies out of business. Smaller companies were eaten by bigger companies. Companies did leveraged buyouts and sold off divisions. Product lines closed. Suddenly people found that the company they had been so loyal to didn't exist any-more, or if it did, it existed in name only as part of a big conglomerate. (And those who work for the new "parent company" often enter the acquired organization with the arrogant demeanor of a conquering army. The "Yeah, you're a general, and I'm just a sergeant, but my company captured your company, so if you want to stay on, it's my way or the highway!" attitude. I've seen it more than a few times, too!)

In the old days, the people who needed résumés were either beginning their careers or planning a big career move. Today, people at all levels of management are needing résumés. Sometimes change has happened so rapidly that people are having to change not just compa-nies, but careers,[36] and they're looking for ways to make all the things they learned in the old career apply to the new. That takes communication skills most of us lack, so we turn to résumé services to help us.

How much do they charge? It depends on how com-plex your résumé is and how much time they spend. Checking in three cities, ranging in size from a half mil-lion to nearly two million, we found that the range was from a low of twenty-five dollars to a high of six hundred dollars. Of course, if you need a job, a better question than "What does it cost to have a professional-looking résumé?" is "What does it cost if I *don't* have a professional-looking résumé?"

....

[36] If you're changing careers or even considering changing careers, check "How to Find an Expert: Career Counselor."

School (Private)

OVERVIEW

The first American schools were set up by the colonists in the early 1600s to teach reading, writing, and religion. They were very strict, very economical, very efficient, very effective, and totally responsible to parents. In 1636, the Massachusetts Bay Colony founded the first college. It was a religious school, called Harvard. The following year, the colony passed a law requiring the establishment of public schools in every town with fifty or more families. Towns with one hundred families were required to set up secondary schools that taught English, the language of the land, along with Latin to prepare students for college. By the 1700s, colonial schools were teaching English, Latin, mathematics, religion, bookkeeping, navigation, and other subjects.

A century after the founding of Harvard, Massachusetts appointed the first state board of education, with Horace Mann as its first secretary. A dozen years later, states began enacting compulsory school attendance laws.

In those days, and up until the middle of this century, public schools were just that—*public* schools, under the control of local school boards which reported

to the parents. Schools reflected the values and standards of the community. Parents believed, rightly, that
the schools were theirs, and the school house was the
center of town, serving as meeting hall and a place for
special events, even religious services.

When I was a small boy, I used to hear old men grum-
ble about the danger of federal aid to education. I well
remember one ancient mcmber of the "whittle and
spit" club proclaiming that the government would put
in just a little of our own tax money and take a lot of
control. Some of the younger men in the circle laughed.
"The government represents the public," they said con-
fidently. "The government would never try to tell us
how to run our local schools."

Well, you may judge for yourself who and what was
right. It seems to me, however, that just as a little rudder
controls a lot of ship, so a little government money controls a lot of education. Many others feel the same way,
and it's not surprising that an ever-increasing number of
parents are opting to remove their children from pub-
lic/government schools into private facilities where they
can influence the curriculum and the faculty. In recognition of this, there were efforts in the Reagan/Bush years
to provide tax credits for parents who put their children
in private schools. The argument was that we are a nation founded on the principles of free enterprise and the
competition would improve *all* schools, both public and
private. Besides, the tax credit was only about half of
what most school districts say it costs them to educate a

child, and taxing experts figured that they were collecting for public schools anyway, and if they returned half that money in a voucher that you could apply to alternative schools, then they'd saved half the cost of educating that child!

Although both Presidents Reagan and Bush favored giving all parents vouchers that would cover all the cost of a "public" school education or could be applied to tuition at private schools, the National Education Association, the union to which most public school teachers belong, fought the idea, and it died.

Still, even without tax vouchers, and although parents must pay for public schools through taxes and private schools out of their pockets, the number of private and even home schools continues to grow. Should you decide to participate in this alternative-yet-traditional educational system, here' s what to look for!

TIPS AND TACTICS

1. Ask around.

Ask friends and neighbors who have children in private schools where their children go, and what they like and dislike about it. If you are looking for a school with a religious affiliation (as nearly all early schools and colleges had), ask at your place of worship. Also, check you local library for a copy of *Peterson's Guide to Private Schools.*

2. Call around.

Call some of the schools that come recommended, and ask questions like these:

Is your school accredited? By whom?

What is your school's philosophy?

What qualifications do you require for teachers? (This will vary from school to school. Christian schools, for instance, might belong to and be accredited by the ACFI. Montessori schools should be affiliated with AMI (American Montessori International). Accreditation by either of these fine organizations requires that teachers have a least a bachelor's degree.

What is your total enrollment? (Beware of schools that are too small. They might not offer adequate recreational and social opportunities.)

How many children are in my child's grade? (Beware of classes that are so small that the children don't have opportunities to interact.)

How many certified teachers do you have? How many in my child's grade? (Look for a good pupil-to-teacher ratio. A class of thirty or more is frequently unmanageable.)

Ask how their students compare on standardized tests with students in public schools.

If the school offers classes through high school, ask what percentage of their students go on to attend college.

3. Visit around.

Visit the schools that seem to offer the most for your child. The campus should be pleasant, the students well mannered and happy looking. The teachers should be in charge, yet approachable. They should be committed to the principles of the school and to your child as an individual. It's a good idea to visit *with* your child, and while you're both there, tour the *entire* school: classrooms, lunchroom, gym, playground, library, etc.

4. Take the shortcut!

If you don't have the time, talent, or inclination to do the foregoing, you *can* opt to find an expert who is specially trained to help you find the right private school for your child. For the last nineteen years, the IECA (Independent Education Consultant's Association) has been helping parents find boarding and day schools for their children. Members are degreed professionals who have a thorough knowledge of the schools available and have visited and examined them personally. They will meet with you and your child, ascertain their academic, social, and emotional needs, recommend a school to meet those needs, and follow his or her progress at the school. They accept no commission from the schools themselves, which makes them totally responsible and responsive to parents. In 1994, one-time fees usually ranged from $500 to $750 for local day schools and $1,200 to $1,500 for boarding schools.

SUMMARY AND CONCLUSION

Our children have attended both private and public schools. While others might have different experiences, the worst private school our children attended was far superior to their best public one. In private school, they received a better education. They received instruction in *values.* They developed better social skills and greater confidence. The teachers listened to them as individuals. The teachers listened to parents as individuals, without our having to resort to organized protests and media events. And why shouldn't teachers and school administrators listen to us parents? In a free enterprise system, serving the needs of customers is a prerequisite to success.

Surveyor (Land)

OVERVIEW

Land surveying has its roots in antiquity. In ancient Egypt, "rope stretchers" came out after each flooding of the Nile to reestablish boundaries for farmers. More than a thousand years before Christ, King Solomon wrote, "Do not move an ancient boundary stone set up by your forefathers." The oldest existing formal treatise on the subject was written by Hero of Alexandria in 250 B.C. By the time of the Roman Empire, surveys were done not just to correctly identify property lines, but prior to building roads, bridges, and aqueducts. In fact, the Romans developed surveying tools and techniques that are still in use today.

Looking for a land surveyor is not unlike looking for a doctor. All are qualified, but many specialize in one or two areas of practice such as loan surveys, acreage tracts, title surveys, topographic surveys, construction surveys, hydrographic surveys, control surveys, and underground surveys. Some surveyors position themselves as "general practitioners" who will take any kind of work. Naturally, you want someone whose specialty is in *the kind of work you want done.*

TIPS AND TACTICS

1. Ask.

This is one of the few fields where the opinions of friends

and neighbors are apt to be misleading. Because there are so many types of surveys, about all friends can tell you is whether or not the surveyor performed on time and on budget. Although this information is good, it is not sufficient to enable you to make a selection. To choose the right surveyor for your job, you need to ask people who are accustomed to dealing with surveyors who do the kind of survey you need. Contact the following and ask them for a *list* of qualified surveyors:

- attorneys who practice real estate law and land boundary litigation
- surveyors who *do not* specialize in your area of need (Yes, most surveyors will be truthful about their own abilities and those of others.)
- the Board of Registration for Professional Land Surveyors
- your state licensing board
- title companies (One surveyor we interviewed felt that title companies were *not* the best source, as he sensed a tendency to opt for surveyors who would mass produce surveys cheaply and rapidly, and sign any certification presented. Evaluate these accordingly, but if a name appears on this list *and* one of your other lists, you might feel greater confidence.)

2. Observe.

Good people in any profession tend to be successful. When you pass a survey crew, note the name on the trucks. Also observe the ads in the Yellow Pages. Most surveyors we interviewed felt that most established firms received most of their business through referrals and consequently ran small ads in the phone directory. "Large ads," one said, "are usually run by new firms hoping to get enough business to stay in business." But while you may disregard the *size* of the ad, you will want to pay close attention to the *ad content.* Look for a surveyor with tenure, one who belongs to the professional associations, and one who is *exclusively* a surveyor. As one surveyor put it, "Some engineering firms do surveying as a sideline. To me, that's akin to a heart specialist doing face-lifts in his spare time. I'd want someone who earned his or her living as a surveyor!"

3. Contact.

Select three names that appeared on more than one list and survived the telephone-book check. Then write up exactly what you need done, send copies to each of the three, and arrange a personal interview. As you interview your surveyor, pay attention to the following:

  appearance of the office
  business acumen
  sources of education
  insured or bonded
■ willingness to work
  personality
  member of the profession's society

Be wary if your surveyor:

  fails to promptly return phone calls
  provides poorly written communication
■ is rude, abrasive, or evasive

fails to ask for a thorough explanation of your problem

refuses to work with your attorney or land title people

is unwilling to enter into a contract for specific performance

asks, "How do you want this survey to come out?"

presses you to make an instant decision

wants to charge an "expedite" fee[37]

4. Investigate.

Ask each surveyor for a list of references for similar work, and call a couple of references from each one. Ask the references if the work was satisfactory, if the billing was at or near the estimate. (If the billing was over the estimate, ask if they were told in advance and if the reason given was satisfactory.)

5. Get a written contract.

If you're dealing with a surveyor you haven't used before, get an agreement in writing that describes your requirements and the fee arrangement. Since surveying is an exact science, most surveyors are very detail oriented and won't mind putting it down in writing. (Besides, you won't be the first one who asked!)

SUMMARY AND CONCLUSION

You wouldn't go to Perry Mason to fight a parking ticket. Unless the stakes are high, you do not have to go to the most expensive and best-known surveyor if you simply want to stake out a sidewalk well within the boundaries

....

[37] One of our sources disagreed with this statement, saying that overtime expenses, etc., were reasonable charges.

of your own property. If for some reason you are unable or unwilling to receive recommendations, construct a list of the things that need to be done, and submit it to three registered professional land surveyors in the area. Ask each for a proposal on how the work should be done. Also, ask for their qualifications, related experience, references, schedule of starting and completing, and a schedule of associated fees. Check a few references and choose the one you think best. Then meet with the surveyor. Does his office appear professional? Does he return phone calls promptly? Does he keep appointments? Is he a member of a professional society? Is he insured and bonded? Do you like him? Is he willing to work? Is he open to your questions. If the answers keep coming up yes—you've got your surveyor!

Swimming Pool Contractor

OVERVIEW

Before you take the *plunge* into a pool purchase, let me share a horror story. A friend of mine decided to have a swimming pool built and selected a contractor who had successfully built several other pools in the area. True, all of those pools had been vinyl lined, and my friend wanted a gunite pool, but he was told by the contractor that the skills were transferable.

During the time the pool was being built, this friend had a lot of illness in his extended family and wasn't around to do much supervision, but the pool was finished on time and looked great. At least, it looked great for a couple of weeks. Then it cracked. Seems the contractor hadn't put rebar in the concrete. And when he wouldn't come and fix it, my friend found the contractor also hadn't placed a ground fault interrupter in the pool

 lights. Eventually, my friend had to hire another contractor to dig up the first pool, haul it off, and build another one. Then, he filed suit against the first contractor to try and recover his money.

At the trial, my friend was awarded the cost of the pool and damages. After the trial, the contractor's attorney approached and said, "We'll settle with you for fifteen hundred dollars." My friend said, "Settle (expletive deleted)! We just won the case!" The contractor's attorney explained, "Yes, but for fifteen hundred dollars he can file bankruptcy. So if you don't take the fifteen hundred, you'll wind up with nothing, because he has no assets."

Although my friend had his day in court *and won*, the best he could negotiate over the threat of bankruptcy was two thousand dollars' cash and a promissory note for one thousand dollars a year for the next five years, about half the cost of the pool.

What became of the contractor who built the shoddy swimming pool? Oh, he moved forty miles away and put in a new business. What kind of business, you ask? He is a swimming pool contractor! Surely, the ancient Persians were right when they wrote, "The *buyer* needs a thousand eyes—the *seller* none."

NOTE: Turn back and read "How to Find an Expert: Building Contractor" and "How to Find an Expert: Remodeler" before checking out the tips and tactics below.

TIPS AND TACTICS

1. Get recent recommendations.
Check with friends who have had their pools long enough to detect problems, say, in the last couple of years. Also, call some pool service companies (who clean

pools and maintain equipment) and ask them who does good work. Then begin checking the names you obtained.

2. Tenure is important.

I would feel more comfortable with a company that had been around for several years . . . enough time for any problems with their earlier pools to show up. I would also feel more comfortable if management had several years' experience *under that name and at that same location.* If management had a lot of experience, but was new, I'd want to know where they had worked before and the name of the company they owned or worked for there.

3. Call the Better Business Bureau.

Ask if they have any complaints against the company. If the management is new, call the BBB at their previous location and check for complaints.

4. Meet with the leading contenders.

The meeting should be friendly, open, and well documented. You should make certain that the bid clearly states:

- that the pool will be built to NSPI (National Spa and Pool Institution) standards for your area
- that the contractor is fully bonded and insured
- that any subcontractors he uses will be bonded and insured
- that the pool and supporting equipment is fully warranted
- that they have a certified service department

5. *Get referrals.*

The best time for any company to obtain referrals is immediately after the work is done. The pool looks beautiful, and the owners can't wait to get into it. My aforementioned friend would have signed a testimonial letter the first week. In getting referrals, make certain that you get some that are "aged." That is to say, get some referrals from folks that *this contractor* built for two to five years earlier. (Of course, if the company has recently changed hands, older references might not be of much value!)

SUMMARY AND CONCLUSION

There are a lot of very reputable, very good swimming pool contractors out there. You need not approach any contractor with a suspicious mind, but you do need to be cautious. You should never feel pressured when you are discussing the purchase of a pool. Neither should you feel that the contractor is being evasive or uncooperative. If you have your own plans and the contractor says, "That can't be done," what he is really saying is, "I don't know how." The only limiting factor to odd-shaped pools should be the cost involved.

The company should have you sign and okay all aspects of putting in the pool and should include a detailed blueprint of the pool, as well as all design elements. I would add "to the best of my knowledge" after my signature. After all, unless you're a professional in the industry, how do you really know it was done correctly?

Never, never, never pay for everything up front. If the payments are to be made in stages, have it clearly understood what completes a stage. Don't be in the position of having paid for 80 percent of the work when only 20 percent has been done. Before making interim or the final payment, require a notarized, signed statement that all their suppliers and subcontractors have been paid for all work they did on this pool and related equipment.

Be cautious when you contract for your pool, and exercise caution when you swim, and you'll have made a purchase that will provide you with many years of enjoyment.

Tile Layer

OVERVIEW

For thousands of years, we've used tile to add strength, beauty, and fire protection to buildings. The old methods of manufacturing and applying tile were so good that many ancient examples remain that are hundreds or even thousands of years old. It's hard to improve on something with that kind of track record, so methods we use today to manufacture and apply tile are similar to those of the ancients.

Tile comes from clay or other earth materials, and when properly mixed and fired (sometimes at temperatures in excess of two thousand degrees), it becomes scratch proof, stain resistant, beautiful, and fireproof. The three most common types of ceramic tile are mosaic, wall, and quarry. Mosaic tiles can be glazed or have color mixed throughout and are usually found on counter tops and light-duty flooring. Wall tiles, which are produced of a porous, neutral-colored material, are color glazed on one side and are used to decorate walls as well as provide an easy-to-clean surface. We frequently find tile walls in hospitals, cafeterias, kitchens, and bathrooms. Quarry tile is larger and stronger than mosaic or wall tile, and is often used for heavy-duty flooring and fireplace hearths.

Marble and slate, though not a tile, are often sold by those who sell tile and are installed by the same craftsmen. (We have a marble-tiled hallway and kitchen that are to die for! Alas, it was put in at the time the house was built and the builder has since passed on, so if I needed a tile layer, I'd be using these tips and tactics, too!)

Tile is often sold these days as a "do-it-yourself" project. Of course, so are kits to build decks, playscapes, gazebos, etc., although some carry a small line of agate copy that says, "Requires basic good carpentry skills." If you have "basic good tile-laying skills," you are welcome to have at it. However, I've learned that while the other person's job might *look* easier than mine, it seldom is. As a friend of mine says, "Bockmon, ain't *nothin'* easy!" To me, the task of removing my old tile, then cutting and properly placing the new, seems fraught with opportunities for disaster. If you are adventurous and have the time, talent, and tenacity, you can get the instructions from your local tile seller and have a go at it. If, like me, you prefer to leave it to the experts (or, if having tried it yourself, you're now ready to ask for help), follow the tips and tactics below and you'll get the person you need.

TIPS AND TACTICS

1. Get recommendations.

On most other professions, we usually began by suggesting you ask friends and neighbors for a recommendation. But let's face it: You're as likely to be abducted by a

UFO as bump into a friend who recently had tile work done! That's because *most* tile work is done in new homes at the time they're built, and it usually lasts until you get tired of looking at it.

Therefore, get recommendations from those who *have* had tile work done recently. I'd suggest you start by calling some of your local builders. Another good bet is to call someplace that sells, but doesn't install, tile. (If you ask someone who sells and installs who they recommend, they will, quite naturally, recommend themselves. Since we rarely judge ourselves as critically as we do others, they are apt to be a bit biased.)

2. Look for someone with tenure.

Once you have their recommendations, check each contractor's ad in the Yellow Pages and see how long they've been at it. (If they don't put how many years they've been in business in the ads, you might assume they haven't been at it long.) Don't be misled by the size of the ads, by the way. Yellow Page advertising is very expensive and the pros in many businesses say, "A lot of new companies start out with big, expensive ads hoping they can get enough business to stay in business. To be successful, they must recoup the cost of the ad by charging a bit more on every job. If they are unsuccessful, and go out of business, who do you call if there's a problem?

3. Look for someone who specializes in tile work.

If tile work is all they do, they'll have to be pretty good at it to survive. If they do tile work, roofing, carpeting, etc., they might be a "jack-of-all-trades and master of none."

4. Call the leading candidates.

Tell them what kind of tile you're wanting to install and ask if that is something they do well. If they say yes, ask them the following:

Can you give me some recent references? (Old references mean they don't do it often!)

I notice in your ad in the phone book that you have _____ years' experience. I realize that's the owner's experience. Will he be laying my tile, or will he send a crew? How much experience will the crew have?

Does your company belong to the Tile Council of America? Why or why not? (The counsel sets standards and answers technical questions. You can call them yourself for a free brochure or a list of members in your area. The telephone number is 609-921-7050.)

Do you use mud-set or thin-set? (Thin-set is faster, but the tile can shift, and thin-set tile should never be used in a shower. Mud takes longer, but also lasts longer. It can even be used to attach tiles to wooden floors.)

5. Ask three companies to come out and give you an estimate.

The estimate should be free, of course. And if you have not selected and purchased your tile previously, you might want them to bring samples. The sample should be identified on the estimate and the cost should include:

ripping out the old tile (if you're replacing)

the cost of the new tile (if you are purchasing tile from them)

laying the new tile

■ all taxes and other costs

It should be understood that tile should never be sanded (it takes the finish off) and if there should be a valid reason for sanding, it should be done prior to installation, as it is a very, very messy process!

You should get a written estimate that lists everything, including ripping out any old tile. Be cautious of anyone who suggests that the new will go right over the old. New tile should not be laid on top of ceramic, wall, or quarry tile, and it is not recommended that it be done on top of vinyl tile.

6. Buy nothing "on the spot."
You will want an opportunity to meet with all the contractors, and if the best was saved until last, you still want to sleep on it. More than that, you want to check each contractor's references by telephone and, if possible, see their work. (We won't say that someone will give you an employee's or a relative's number, but it could happen.)

SUMMARY AND CONCLUSION

Tile layers in my state aren't licensed. If they are licensed in your state, find out what the license means, because oftentimes licenses are designed as a revenue-enhancement program and not to guarantee work to a common standard. Still, a license is some kind of protection, in that you could always protest its renewal if you got a bad job. All this points out that you need to be very careful about whom you select. I'd be apprehensive of anyone who:

■ tried to collect in advance (I might be persuaded to

pay for the tile, upon delivery, but the remaining balance is upon completion. For information on why, check "How to Find an Expert: Building Contractor" and "How to Find an Expert: Fencing Contractor.")

■ told me the tile would be perfectly level (The little imperfections and differences are what make tile beautiful.)

■ doesn't offer a written guarantee of tile and labor

■ doesn't make eye contact

■ couldn't answer questions, yet didn't offer to find out the answers

■ doesn't make me feel comfortable

Tile laying is a craft, and the lowest price probably won't come from the best craftsman. A very low price speaks of desperation or inexperience. A very high price might say, "I've really got all the work I can handle." On the other hand, one craftsman might be considerably more expensive than another who is equally as good, so compare not only prices but quality.

Tanning Salon

OVERVIEW

When the rays of the sun strike our skin, they cause an increase in pigmentation. This phenomenon is called "tanning." People who work, play, or lay in the sun therefore get tanned as a natural consequence. However, natural tanning takes patience and planning. If we get in a hurry and get too much sun too fast, we get sunburn, which can cause redness, blistering, burning, and then the peeling off of the very tan we were so proud of! While light-skinned people are more likely to suffer sunburn than dark-skinned ones, anyone can burn if exposed to enough ultraviolet light rays. The problem is compounded because many people don't realize that ultraviolet passes right through clouds and fog, so you can burn on a day when you don't even see the sun. In addition, ultraviolet waves reflect quite nicely off sand and even snow—so you can sunburn even when it's freezing outside!

To avoid burning in the sun, many people use protective sunscreens that block ultraviolet B light (UVB). However, these sunscreens do very little to shield your skin from ultraviolet A (UVA), and on a sunny day, more than 90 percent of the ultraviolet light that lands on our skin is UVA, which is just as likely to cause skin cancer as UVB. In fact, Dr. Robert Atkins, in his *Health Revelations Newsletter* (August 1994), asks, "Could this be why skin cancer rates in the United States, Canada, Australia, and Scandinavia—the countries that use the most sunscreen—have risen steadily?"

Atkins says that users of sunscreen might put themselves at risk for two reasons. One, because they are blocking UVB, they tend to stay out in the sun longer and two, the UVB that is being blocked promotes our body's production of vitamin D, which has been shown to suppress the growth of melanoma cells. Atkins suggests that we leave the sunscreen use at home unless necessary and enjoy the sun in moderation, tanning slowly to avoid scorching our skin.

Since most people[38] associate a nice suntan with good health, and many want a nice, hassle-free tan even in winter without the risk or inconvenience of lying in the sun, tanning salons have become quite popular. Our daughter Rebecca visits such a salon frequently. While everyone admits that she has a great-looking tan, she is quick to point out that some of the other patrons of her tanning parlor have such a deep tan that, in her words, "They look like mahogany furniture." Not having seen them, I can't comment on the accuracy of her description, but I have seen one newsman on TV whose face is dark enough to be a mahogany mask—except for the white circles around the eyes where his UV goggles go!

If you want a great year-round tan, here's how to go

....

[38] Except dermatologists, many of whom say that overexposure to the sun can not only damage the skin now, but might contribute to skin cancer later in life!

about finding a tanning salon that will work with you and work to protect you at the same time!

TIPS AND TACTICS

1. Visit places near you.

Many offer a free first tan. If so, use this as an opportunity to look around. If not, call a nearby place and ask to examine the premises. The facility should be neat and clean and fully insured to cover any injuries.

2. They should have rules about tanning.

Tanning in a salon might be safer than tanning under the sun. However, ultraviolet light can still cause sunburn if guidelines aren't obeyed. Their rules should be similar to these:

- Each person should be given an individual evaluation before his first tan.

- We will begin with just a few minutes on a tanning bed and gradually increase the length of time. Usually, the increase comes every third visit and can be extended no more than two minutes at a time.

- We will watch you for any redness, and particularly any redness that lasts more than a day.

- We will reduce your exposure if you experience redness.

- We will sanitize the beds after each use.

- We will show you a sign-out sheet that states the bed was sanitized after the last use.

- We will change lamps regularly. (Those we spoke with recommended at least every eight hundred hours.)

3. Ask about fees.

Most places offer monthly rates with discounts for longer memberships. Annual memberships, at most places, cost about the same as ten monthly memberships. (However, I wouldn't pay for a full year *in advance*, unless they could convince me that they'd be in business a *full year*!) In addition, many salons offer "specials"—particularly in the summer when business is slower.

4. Find a place that takes appointments.

Your time is valuable, or you'd be sunning outside in the summer instead of visiting a tanning salon. Don't waste it just because you came at a crowded time. However, if you don't mind waiting, you also can look for a place that will try to "fit you in" without an appointment.

5. You should be able to tan comfortably.

The better beds have radios and fans, and the better salons have private rooms and great air conditioning. (Hey, if you wanted to sweat, you'd go outside, right?)

SUMMARY AND CONCLUSION

A good tanning salon is very, very concerned about your health. They would rather lose a customer by refusing to extend tanning times than risk your health by allowing to overcook. But, unless you want to be followed by termites, don't tan until you look like furniture, or your skin takes on the texture of leather.

Travel Agency

OVERVIEW

Before the deregulation of the airline industry, I only used travel agents when I was going to some city I'd never visited and didn't know where to stay. After all, rates for air travel and rental cars were pretty much standard and well known. Today, however, there seems to be no set price for anything and traveling in America is like traveling in a third-world country: You have to haggle price on everything you buy, from airline tickets to rent cars to hotel rooms.[39]

....

[39] I once teased an airline executive that four dozen "executive terrorists" armed with two bottles of champagne each could destroy the domestic airline industry in twenty-four hours. When challenged, I explained, "Each executive would board a different domestic flight. Once the plane was in the air, he would stand and say, 'Ladies and Gentlemen, I'm going to give a bottle of champagne to the passenger who paid *the most* for his or her ticket!' He would then ask for a show of hands for who paid more than seven hundred dollars, then eight hundred dollars, then eight hundred fifty and so on. The one who paid the most would get the bottle of champagne."

The airline exec was puzzled. "I don't see how that would disrupt air travel."

I replied, "No, because all the passengers would be feeling smug that some schmuck had overpaid for his ticket—but don't forget, each terrorist has *another* bottle of champagne! Now, he announces that he will give a bottle of champagne to the passenger who paid the least for his ticket! He'd start at five hundred dollars and work his way down. When passengers who had paid six, seven or eight hundred dollars discovered that others had paid two or three hundred for a ticket on the same flight, they'd riot and destroy the aircraft!"

The airline executive hearing my tale hurriedly changed the subject, murmured something about me being dangerous, and shoved a handful of free drink coupons at me. He was uneasy because rates are a sticky issue with airlines, and he knew my story was based on solid fact. In a single month, I flew round-trip coach class (a/k/a "last class") from Dallas, Texas, to Charlotte, North Carolina, three times. On none of those occasions did I pay the same for a ticket. The *lowest-priced ticket* was $188. The *highest-priced ticket* was $850! Had there been an "executive terrorist" on board those flights, I would have arrived home with two bottles of champagne.

For many months, I frequently traveled the same Dallas-to-Charlotte-to-Dallas route, and depending upon the kind of deal I got, the price of a round-trip ticket varied from less than two hundred to more than eight hundred dollars. (It was eight hundred when they were promoting six days and five nights in London *including airfare and hotel for six hundred dollars!*). The point is, today's airline pricing is so complex and there are so many exclusions and options that it really takes a seasoned professional to sort them all out. Enter, the professional travel agent.

A travel agent costs you nothing, as they're paid a commission from airlines, rental car companies, and hotels. Since their success depends upon making you happy, a good agent will not only get you the best price going, but will see that you go in the style to which you are accustomed. I am accustomed to going in coach or "last class," squeezed into tiny seats made for skinny, short people. I do, however, try to get an aisle seat, so I can have circulation in at least one arm (except when the beverage cart is in the aisle, people are walking up and down, etc.). Once I'm on terra firma, I feel like a POW coming out of a tiger cage, and want nothing more than to stretch out and find the person who designed the torture chamber I just exited. Once I leave the airport (many of which have replaced bus stations for sleaziness), I want a bit of luxury. To me, that means a full-sized automobile and a nice hotel with a good restaurant that has reserved me a king-sized bed in a nonsmoking room. A good travel agent can get me all of that—at the best rate going.

Whatever it is that *you* want, a good travel agent can and will do that for you—reliably. A poor agent will just call and get you on the next flight out, forget your preferences, and try to find an excuse that includes you among the guilty if you complain. I've had both. Here's how to go about getting a good travel agent!

TIPS AND TACTICS

1. Get recommendations.

If you don't travel much, get recommendations from friends who do. Ask:

　Does this agent give personal service and keep a permanent record of your likes and dislikes?

　Does the agency have a lot of turnover among employees?

　Is the agency tied to one airline and hotel chain, or do they try to get you the best schedule, rate, and property at each location?

■ Does the agency return your calls promptly?

　Does the agency keep you on hold?

■ Does the agency deliver what they promise?

　Does the agency admit their mistakes and try to correct them?

　Does the agency seem familiar with the destinations you choose?

　Do they have an 800 number? (If you have a problem on the road, it would be nice to be able to call them without having to drop coins in a pay phone for twenty minutes.)

Does the agent issue tickets and boarding passes? (You always want to arrive at the airport with a ticket in hand so you can check your bags at the curbside check-in. You do not want to wind your way through a maze, pushing your bags ahead of you, to pick up your ticket or boarding pass!)

Where is the agency? (If you live in a large metropolitan area and have to pick up tickets for a quick trip, location can be very important!)

2. Call the agencies.

Call each agent and each agency that got high marks. Tell who recommended them, explain that you do not need a reservation *at this time*, but you do travel (often, frequently, occasionally) on (business, pleasure, etc.,) and would like to choose a new agent. The agent, in anticipation of your business, should ask you a lot of questions for their file so they will be better able to help you. They'll want to know:

What airlines, rental car, and hotel chains do you prefer?

What frequent flyer, frequent lodger, etc., clubs do you belong to?

Do you qualify for a corporate rate?

Is schedule more important than air carrier?

Where do you like to sit on an airplane?

What kind of hotel accommodations do you prefer?

How much advance notice do you usually have before

you travel? (Advance notice often enables them to obtain a better rate.)

3. Talk to at least three agencies.

Go with the one that seems the most caring and competent.

SUMMARY AND CONCLUSION

Travel agents handle both business and recreational travel. Some specialize in one or the other, but most handle both, though they handle them differently.

■ Business Travel

When you're traveling on business, the most important thing is *accuracy.* If you have a meeting at two o'clock in the Exxon Building at 800 Bell Street in Houston, Texas, you and your travel agent realize you can't take a chance on a missed connection leading to a missed meeting. Therefore, they will make every effort to get you on a flight early enough that even normal airline screwups won't affect your schedule.

They'll also give more consideration to the *convenience* factor than they do to the *cost* factor. If your meeting is in town, this means you'll probably be staying in a much more expensive hotel with smaller rooms and fewer amenities than you would if traveling on pleasure.

■ Recreational travel

When we travel for pleasure, it's *our* money instead of company money we're spending, so a good travel agent will often give more weight to *cost* than to

convenience. After all, if you can reduce your hotel bill
by 40 percent by driving six miles to Disneyworld
rather than two, they'll at least ask you if it isn't worth
it. They'll also look for ways to help you reduce your
transportation cost, even if it means flying by a somewhat circuitous route and picking up a rental car off
the airport property.[40] They'll often go even further to
help you by researching various "vacation packages"
that combine hotel, air travel, rental cars, and tickets
to nearby amusement areas to save you money.

There is an illusion, fostered by airlines, that air travel is
fast. Actually, only air*craft* are fast, air *travel* is slow. No
plane ever leaves on time. No plane ever arrives on time.
Even before you get to the airport, you have a long drive
ahead of you, the car has to be parked or turned in. Bags
have to be checked. Boarding passes have to be obtained
(though most travel agents can issue these at the time
they deliver your tickets). Then there is a long wait for
the aircraft you'll be boarding to actually arrive. You will
have to line up to get onto the plane. Airlines keep cram-
ming in more and more rows of seats so that even
munchkins complain of no legroom, so you'll be uncomfortable. Then you'll eventually back away from the
gate and your aircraft will be number seventy-four for

....

[40] I personally wouldn't pay a nickel more to get a car on the airport property than I
would to get a car off the property. If you go up to a counter in the airport, you stand
in line, fill out the paperwork, then catch a shuttle to the remote area where your car
is waiting. If you get a car off the airport property, you catch a shuttle to the remote
area, stand in line, fill out the paperwork, and pick up your car. It seems to me that
it's six one way and a half dozen the other. Except that off-premises rental cars are
usually less expensive.

takeoff. At last, you'll get airborne. The captain will get on the intercom, and forgetting that they've put in eight more rows of seats since he last flew coach, will tell people to "lean back and relax." Your knees are already touching the seat back in front of you. A seven-foot man weighing an eighth of a ton will lean back, effectively placing his head in your lap. When the food comes, you will have to try and eat it with your elbows touching your sides because there is no room to move because your elbows must remain at your side or you're poking your seat mates in the stomach. So it's sort of like eating with your upper arms lashed to your body, which is quite difficult. Besides, once you taste the food, you realize it isn't worth the effort. Compared to what's served today in the air, McDonald's is a four-star restaurant!

There isn't much we can do about the dismal state of domestic air travel. We've come a long way from the days when a dinner flight meant you'd be enjoying steak and a good wine, when you could stretch out and relax, or go to the lounge and play cards, and when jets were called "luxury jets" and "pamper jets." Those days are gone with ten-cent sodas and poodle skirts and "Nixon's the One!" buttons. Nothing can be done to bring them back—but with a good travel agent, you can at least be assured that you'll make your connections and that everything that can be done for you will be done for you. And think of that nice car and that nice big bed waiting for you on the ground!

Veterinarian

Veterinary medicine has been with us a long, long time. Cave dwellers practiced veterinary medicine on their dogs by removing splinters, immobilizing broken bones, cooling fevered bodies, and bringing food and water to their sick pets. Four thousand years ago, the Code of Hammurabi set regulations for the practice of medicine on both humans and animals. Nineteen hundred years ago, Greek physicians dissected animals to learn how their bodies worked and contributed greatly to the storehouse of veterinary knowledge.

Considering the long, illustrious, and rich history of the veterinary profession, it seems almost unbelievable that the first veterinary school didn't appear until 1761. *The first American school didn't open until the Civil War!* Still, in the short time today's professional vets have been on the scene, they've chalked up an impressive list of victories, including the eradication of hoof-and-mouth disease, Texas Tick Fever, and anthrax, while bringing diseases such as brucellosis, hog cholera, distemper, and rabies under control.

Considering that physicians sometimes have difficulty

diagnosing our ailments, although we can describe the symptoms, it is amazing how well veterinarians do dealing with animals that lack the power of reasoned speech! Veterinary knowledge doesn't come easily—or quickly. Today's vet has seven years of education (more, if he specializes) and a sizable capital investment in establishing a medical practice. All veterinarians are well educated and well trained, but like other professionals, some are even better than others. Here's how to go about finding your own veterinary expert!

TIPS AND TACTICS

1. Check around.

Ask other pet owners and groomers to recommend a vet to you, or call the American Veterinary Association and ask them to recommend a vet in good standing in your area. Vets, like physicians, may be a "general practitioner" or may specialize by types of animals (dogs and cats, farm animals, horses, exotics, etc.) or types of problems (general medicine, surgery, geriatrics, ultrasound, orthopedics, cardiology, radiology, dermatology, etc.). Usually, as with human illnesses, it's best to begin with a good general practitioner and let him recommend a specialist should one be needed.

2. Call around.

Explain that you're looking for a veterinarian for your pet and would like some information. Some questions you should ask are:

■ How many years has Dr. _____ been in practice?

>   (This is important because you want experience, but
>   you don't want to go to the trouble of finding a vet only
>   to find that he is retiring in a few months![41])

Is this a general practice, or do you specialize in certain types of animals?

What are your hours?

What are your fees for office visits, inoculations, etc.?

What provisions do you have for after-hour care?

Are you certified by the American Animal Hospital Association (AAHA)?

Is the veterinarian board certified as to any specialty?

Will you notify me when routine care is needed?

3. Visit a vet.

If you've planned ahead and are trying to locate a suitable veterinarian before he is needed, take an afternoon and visit a few clinics. The office should be clean, reasonably free of odors (we all know that excited canines sometimes lose bladder control!), and cheerful looking, and the staff friendly. You should be able to check an examining room and have a few moments to chat with the vet. Remembering that he is busy, you'll want to make your visit brief. Still, you should find him helpful, polite, and open, able to convey confidence.

4. Choose your vet.

Once you've chosen, it's a good idea to take your pet in for a checkup *before* there is a problem. This way, the vet

----

[41] One of the DVMs we interviewed said that years in practice isn't the sole measure of capability; if the vet is in a group practice, experience is mixed with new knowledge and techniques, giving you the best of both worlds.

can get to know the animal, note its normal weight, etc., do any diagnostic tests required (such as for heart-worm), and prescribe any preventative medicines that might be required. By doing this, you will not only have done all you can to safeguard your pet's health, but you will have performed the introductions between pet and vet under relaxed circumstances.

SUMMARY AND CONCLUSION

"The proof of the pudding," the adage goes, "is in the eating thereof." Once you've selected your vet, the proof you've chosen wisely will be in his performance. Animals in pain respond well to a kind word and a gentle touch—just as people do. Therefore, when you take your pet in, the vet should treat it gently and kindly, and should talk to it in a soothing manner.

Naturally, the purpose of your visit to the vet is either to keep your pet well or help it get well. Unless your animal has a fatal disease, you should expect improvement as a result of the treatment.

In our section on doctors, we said, "Many physicians order tests not because they're needed for a diagnosis, but to protect themselves against a charge of not having exercised 'due diligence' in providing health care." Many vets *hesitate* to order tests to confirm a diagnosis because they are concerned that the cost of the test will exceed the cost of trying several courses of treatment. (If the vet is dealing with a farm animal, it's a rather simple calculation to balance the value of the animal against the cost of the test. However, when the patient is a beloved animal companion, you will have to let him know if you'd prefer a battery of tests to try and solve the problem faster, and whether or not you want exotic and expensive treatments for a heart condition or cancer.)

Still, a good vet, like a good doctor, will put all the cards on the table and let you decide from the options. However, if prolonged treatment hasn't been effective, and the vet doesn't suggest tests or refer you to a specialist, it's up to you to broach the subject. If the vet still won't authorize the test or a referral, then you'll probably need to go through the procedure of locating a vet all over again.

Wedding Consultant

OVERVIEW

According to the book of Genesis, the first wedding took place in a garden, and God Himself gave the bride away. There's never been a wedding that impressive, but over the centuries, weddings have become more and more complex. (After all, Eve didn't have a mother and aunts to help plan the extravaganza!) Naturally, the bride and groom need to be there, as well as their parents, their relatives, and their friends. Also, you need someone to perform the ceremony. It's also a good idea to have a good photographer on hand to record it all, because the bride and groom are in a daze, and, someday, when they come down from cloud nine, they'll want to see what they missed. You'll also need caterers and musicians or at least a pianist. Florists, of course, are essential. The groom, groomsmen, and the fathers of both the bride and groom will need tuxes. The mother of the groom and the mother of the bride will need new dresses, and, naturally, they want to coordinate with the bridesmaids, who will need new dresses, too. Well, the list of people, and things, and professionals you'll need is almost endless.

Time was when the mother of the bride and the immediate family did most of the planning for most weddings. Today, the mother of the bride is likely to be working nine to five herself and will have neither the time nor the knowledge required to make her daughter's storybook romance end in a storybook wedding. This is the cue for the entrance of the professional wedding consultant, someone who can say, "Been there; done that," and "This is what we need to do."

You want a wedding consultant who can handle all the little details that go into making it all happen and one who can listen to the family's wishes, modify things to fit, and still make everything come off on time, on target, and on budget. It's a big order! Here's how to fill it!

TIPS AND TACTICS

1. First, ask yourself if you really need a wedding consultant.

If you have time, if you have experience, if you know who to contact for all the elements that go into a wedding, then you might wish to do it yourself. You need to make this decision firmly and finally before you proceed.

2. Get referrals from newlyweds.

Once you've decided that you need (or want) help, you might begin your task of finding the right wedding consultant. If you have friends who've recently had weddings in their family, ask if they used a wedding consultant, and if so, if they were pleased. If you don't have any friends who married recently, ask if *they* have any family or friends who did, and work from there. Your minister, priest, or rabbi would also be a good source of leads, as would any of the places where the wedding party will meet. When you have *at least* three names on your list, proceed to step three.

3. Contact the candidates with the best recommendations.

Tell them that they have been recommended by _____ and that you are planning a wedding on such and such date. Ask if they are available. (There's really no reason to prolong the conversation otherwise.) If they are, ask questions like these:

■ How much experience do you have? There are no generally recognized fields of study to create wedding consultants.[42] Therefore, the way this person comes across to you will be very important. You need to know how he got into the wedding consulting business. He needs to present himself as well organized, methodical, yet personable and open to your suggestions and questions. Remember: if you don't feel comfortable with this person *now* when there is none of the last-minute pressure and hassle of a wedding, you certainly won't when you get "down to the wire."

■ Do you handle everything? (If you wish to handle part of the preliminary or postwedding events yourself, make that clear. However, you are opening yourself up for misunderstandings if you split responsibilities at any single event.)

....

42 However, membership in organizations like ABC (Association of Bridal Consultants), Meeting Planners International, or the National Association of Catering Executives would be an encouraging sign.

■ If you handle everything, are you responsible for everything? That is, will you oversee everything from the wedding cake to the wedding photos?

■ How do you charge? This seems to vary by region. In the Northeast, it seems that many wedding consultants charge a percentage of the total fee. In the South and West, they most often work off a flat rate. What you don't want is a fee plus hourly charges so that the meter is running during rehearsals, etc. Ask if they receive a commission or percentage from those they recommend. If they do, you will want to be certain that they've selected the best for the money, not just the one who pays the biggest percentage.

■ Could you give me some recent references? True, you called them because someone referred them. But for all you know, that might have been "one-in-a-row."

4. Check the references.

Get at least three references from each of your three wedding consultants. (I know, this takes a lot of time, but once you've found the right person, think of how much time and hassle you'll save!) Ask each of the references what he liked *best* and *least* about his or her wedding consultant.

5. Call the leading candidate.

Tell him that you are strongly considering using him and ask if he offers a free initial consultation. Go and meet with the consultant, and if you feel comfortable, iron out the details. There is even software available to assist you and your consultant in planning the myriad details involved in your wedding.

6. Get everything in writing.

Most people are honest, but most people occasionally forget. Wedding consultants usually offer tiered packages that spell out what is included in writing. If none of these fit your needs, then they can create a custom package for you, again detailing just what you're getting and just what you will be paying. Speaking of payment, it is customary to pay half the consultant's fee up front as a retainer with the balance to be paid either the night of the rehearsal or the day of the wedding. However, make it a habit not to pay for anything else in advance. Whenever possible, pay only as, or after, the service is rendered, and pay from itemized invoices.

7. Once you've picked the consultant, let the consultant be the consultant.

Sure, it's your wedding, and you have a right to input, but if you have confidence in the person, don't micromanage the wedding. Relax. Enjoy the moment, because there's a fifty-fifty chance that you'll never have to arrange another wedding with this person.

SUMMARY AND CONCLUSION

There is something wonderful about love and marriage. As the old song went, "They go together like a horse and carriage!" In spite of the fact that guys kid about weddings being "walking funerals," most of us hairy-chested males like weddings, too. There's something nice about two people pledging to live their lives as one, about two families being brought together, about solemn and happy vows being undertaken in the words from the traditional marriage ceremony:

Dearly beloved, we are gathered together here in the sight of God, and in the presence of these witnesses, to join together this man and this woman in holy matrimony; which is an honorable estate, instituted of God in the time of man's innocence, signifying unto us the mystical union that is between Christ and His Church. . . .

If you're planning a wedding, may I add my congratulations to those who know and love you better!

Weight-Loss Consultant

I am a fat person. Not *pleasingly plump*, not *stout*, not *beefy*—fat. I am with eating as Mark Twain was with smoking. He said that it wasn't hard to quit smoking, he had quit hundreds of times. I quit smoking in 1975. It was hard, but I just didn't smoke. I didn't place pipe or cigar or cigarette in my mouth. You can do that with alcohol or smoking, but not with food. I mean, you have to eat, or you die. (Okay, it would take some of us a loonnnnggg time to die after we stopped eating!) Once you start eating, it's so easy to say, "Pass me another helping of those mashed potatoes!" or "Cut me another slice of chocolate pie!"

The preceding paragraph made me hungry just writing it! "Heaven," my portly friend Craig Lacy says, "is never having to say you're full!" (Incidentally, Craig makes the best bread pudding in the world. He starts with homemade biscuits! I hope, when my time to die comes, I arrive in heaven with the taste of that bread pud still in my mouth!)

Over the years, I've successfully dieted, and like most people, once the diet was off, the weight was back on.

I've tried low-calorie foods, low-calorie diets, carbohy-drate diets, protein diets, and diet pills. Diet pills would work if the reason most of us ate was because we were hungry. The fact is, most of us larger folks eat because it tastes good, or we're busy, or we're bored. Unfortunately, one of those reasons is always at hand.

I've come to the conclusion that we all do basically what we want to do. I'm fat because, although I *don't re-ally* want to be fat, I want to be fat more than I want to cut down on my eating! I eat in full knowledge that, "A moment upon the lips means forever upon the hips." If you're fat, it's because you want to be fat, too. That is, you prefer the consequences of overeating more than you prefer the consequences of eating less fattening foods, eating smaller portions, and exercising more.[43] *We are what we are because of the decisions we have made.*

If *you have decided* that you want to look and feel bet-ter more than you want to eat what you want, you can lose weight and keep it off. However, this cannot be ac-complished by a *program* that has a start and a stop date. You must commit yourself to a *system* that continues to work day after day. There must be a change not only in your eating habits, but your lifestyle. If you're ready to make that kind of commitment, you *could* just pick up a good book on nutrition and eat smaller portions of less-fattening food. However, we all know it's easier to change

....

[43] It's the kind of half-hearted commitment Oscar Wilde wrote about in his play, *A Woman of No Importance.* "To win back my youth . . . there is nothing I wouldn't do, except take exercise, get up early, or be a useful member of the community."

when others are on the team with us, rooting for us, coaching us, helping us with the day-to-day struggle. So if you decide you want to be thin again, or for the first time, here's how to find pros that will help you lose weight. You read this while I go fix a cup of hot cocoa. Some of those miniature marshmallows would be nice on top, don't you think?

TIPS AND TACTICS

1. Beware of things new.

Fad diets and fad diet plans come out all the time. Those not backed by a multilevel marketing organization are featured just about every other month in health, fitness, and women's magazines. Invariably, most are found to be overpriced, and some are later found to be either lacking in nutrition or even dangerous. Since our friends are as likely to be caught up in these things as anyone else, put your mind in the "sounds suspicious to me mode" before you move to step two.

2. Ask friends.

We are so concerned with being politically correct these days that conversation can become stilted. A male friend, who works for a major, multinational corporation, was at a social gathering where a female co-worker was present. After a bit of chitchat, he said, rather hesitantly, "You really are looking good these days." She laughed and said, "Thank you! I've been on a diet for three weeks, and no one has said *anything*. I was afraid no one even noticed." The friend said, "Well, to tell the truth, the company is so concerned about sexual harassment complaints that we're not supposed to comment on how female workers look. In fact, I was a little hesitant to mention it even off premises."

If you have a friend who has lost weight and who won't feel harassed by your commenting, ask him what he's doing and where he's doing it! (If your friend does feel harassed, turn back and read "How to Find an Expert: Attorney.")

3. Interview some firms.

Select some names that have been recommended and go in for an interview. While no firm will do all the things listed below, good ones will do some of the following:

- obtain health information from you before recommending any change
- get a clearance from your physician before entering you into their program
- belong to or work with the American Dietetic Association (ADA-approved programs teach you good nutrition as well as calorie counting.)
- have counselors who have overcome weight problems themselves (This enables them to have empathy and to give better support. This might not always be possible, as there must be some law that would be violated if a weight-loss clinic tried to only hire the formerly fat. The always thin might think it was job discrimination.)
- have counselors who have some psychological training as well

- tell you the truth—that healthy weight loss doesn't happen quickly, easily, or without a total, lifetime commitment
- recommend a plan that is flexible, fits into your lifestyle, is easy to follow, and has good food that *you enjoy*
- help you discover what triggers you to eat

4. Find out what it all costs.

There are a lot of nice business people in America, but few of them went into business just to be nice. Just about all of them went into business *with the intention* of making a profit. Find out what the whole program costs. Beware of "loss leaders" such as, "Lose all the weight you want for $X!" This is usually just a start-up fee, and they expect you to buy foods, supplements, etc. Even if you buy the whole package, no one can guarantee your continued success. A certain celebrity lost a lot of weight, and her diet was highly advertised and touted . . . until the weight began to come back. Since I am a firm believer in the principle that people do what they want to do, the only way I can think of that they can guarantee your weight loss would be to lock you in a cage. Since that would be illegal, they usually footnote such claims with a "provided the client rigidly follows the diet and exercise program." An exclusion like that pretty well makes it meaningless, doesn't it?

5. Include your local hospital on your list!

Many hospitals offer excellent weight-loss programs that include behavior modification and nutritional training. The cost can be very competitive with others in the business.

SUMMARY AND CONCLUSION

I make it a habit to never sign a contract while I'm excited. I like to take it home, read it, and think on it a few days. Then, if I have questions, I can get them answered *before* it's too late. If any place you talk with is uncomfortable with that, then it is obvious that they are more interested in making a sale than providing a service. I would avoid anyone who refused to answer questions or who said, "I'll get back to you on that" and didn't. Avoid anyone who was rude, pushy, or condescending. If you're entering into a weight-loss contract with someone, it's important that both parties respect the other. Fortunately, there are some good weight-loss consultants out there who have wonderful track records for helping people who *really want to lose weight.* If you are really committed to losing weight, following the tips and tactics from our experts should help you find the right one for you.

Writer

OVERVIEW

I have earned my living as a writer since 1976, and I'm always amazed that those who don't write think it's so easy. Perhaps that is because a number of myths have centered on the craft. Since I write for both publication (articles, books, plays, etc.) and for business (brochures, speeches, corporate sales, safety and training videos, etc.), we'll begin by exposing some myths in each field.

WRITING FOR PUBLICATION
Myth #1: All it takes is a good idea.
At every party, *at least one person* will come to me and say, "I've got a great idea for a story. Why don't I tell you about it, you write it, and we'll split the money?" Anyone can have ideas, it's doing something with them that takes talent.
Myth #2: If you can type, you can write.
In her "autobiography," singer Reba McEntire gushes, "We selected Tom Carter . . . to be the co-author. Tom did a great job interviewing people, gathering all the facts, listening to all the endless stories, and *typing it all up.*" See, if *you* had learned to type like Tom, you could be a coauthor, too!
Myth #3: All it takes is time.
Writing for publication takes time, talent, and

tenacity. Two of the three aren't sufficient. Oftentimes, even having all three isn't enough.

WRITING FOR BUSINESS
Myth #1. Anybody can do it.
Since business writing requires clear, concise writing, myths abound that anyone who can write a clear, concise letter can also write a clear, concise brochure, speech, video script, or seminar. That's akin to saying, "Anyone who can sew can be a surgeon." Each business communications device is separate and distinct, and requires special skills. You're either going to have to find an expert in the company who knows the material and teach him to write well, or find a skilled writer and put him in touch with the subject-matter expert. The latter course is easier.
Myth #2. Writing is writing.
Some people feel that a writer is a writer is a writer, and a writer who can write one type of material can easily write another. That's not necessarily so. Just because your writer does a great job on a technical manual, it does not follow that he can also do a great job on your corporate video. To write effectively for video or film, the writer must know the media, just as to write and design a brochure or manual, he must understand printing; and to write a speech, he must understand audiences.
Myth # 3. It's not important that the writer know your business.
A good writer will conduct interviews to learn about your business, your competition, your people, and your needs

to help you. You could probably provide *all* of that data, but there's nothing quite as helpful as having a writer who has gained some independent knowledge of the matter beforehand by working on similar projects for similar companies.

TIPS AND TACTICS

1. Find a writer who fits your need.
A writer with experience in many media and experience in many businesses may offer a veritable feast of fantastic credentials. However, your primary need is for a writer who knows *your* business and who can translate your message to the medium best suited for your audiences and your budget.

As H. Holland (Dutch) Harpool says, "Few writers can handle both the spoken and the written word. If yours can't and your project requires both, then you'll need to assemble a compatible team, perhaps with a different member handling video, speeches, and printed material."

2. Find a full-time professional.
A writer, by definition, is "one who writes." A lot of people write, but very few make a living doing it. While you may luck into a gifted amateur, you'll have a better shot at success if you find a writer who earns his entire living writing. Professionals will have the experience, training, dedication, and skills necessary to guide you and your project to a successful conclusion. How do you find that writer? "Therein," as Shakespeare said, "lies the rub."

Writers rely on personal contact and recommendations by other clients. Still, you might begin with the Yellow Pages. For better sources:

- ■ call ad agencies and ask for recommendations
- ■ call video production companies and ask for recommendations
- ■ call the local library and ask if there are any professional, full-time writers in your area
- ■ call any large corporations in your area, ask to speak to the public relations department, and ask them for recommendations

3. Have reasonable expectations.

Once you have a list of writers to contact, you need to find one that can turn out copy that's on target, on time, and on budget. However, the copywriter is not a public relations expert, and cannot guarantee that you're going to get free publicity or a book or movie contract as a result of his work. Copy has to be *sold*. That's why most writers who write for public relations agencies don't handle media relations, and those who write for publication, television, or motion pictures usually have literary agents.

A good presentation or a great video can help make a poor salesperson better and a good one great—but whenever the subject is complex, the competition stiff, or a substantial investment is required, a well-trained salesman must be there to close the sale. Your written sales and marketing material can "soften the target" and "ease the sale," but it can't do the job alone.

4. Interview writers who come recommended.

Pay particular attention to those who:

- have earned their living by writing for a number of years
- can "name drop" important projects for important clients
- have specific experience in your industry and in the medium you wish to use
- ask pointed questions about the project: the purpose, the audience, the message, the goal, what the audience thinks and feels now, and what you want them to think and feel after being exposed to your message
- can produce samples of their work (However, as you look at the samples, concentrate on the *writing,* not on the presentation. Good graphic design can disguise ineffective writing to the cursory reader. Learn to look beyond the packaging and study the writing. The writing samples you see and hear should educate, entertain, and motivate the target audience to action.)

5. Write up an agreement.

Your writer should provide you with a written estimate that describes what will be done and what it will cost. It should say plainly that the budget will not exceed that amount *unless* something happens that you both agree in writing should affect the price.

If you're looking for a coauthor for a book, unless you're famous and have publishers nipping at your heels, expect not only to share any advances and royalties, but also plan to pay the writer a fee up front to cover the cost of researching and writing the book proposal.

6. Follow the advice of your professional.

At the beginning of any business or book project, when all seems confused, muddled, and disorganized, everyone is quite content to let the writer be the writer and stay out of the way. As the project begins to take final form, however, all the latent desires to write start coming to the surface. As author H. G. Wells said, "No passion in the world is equal to the passion to alter someone else's draft."

Professional writers should give their business clients what they need, consistent with what they will approve and pay for. As a professional business writer, I understand that my clients know more about their business than I ever will, so I listen to their advice and take their suggestions seriously. However, I know more about writing for business than they do. Therefore, if I think they are making a mistake, I will try to convince them not to do it. As a professional author, I encourage coauthors not to make and editors not to take changes that haven't filtered through the primary writer, because a written piece should be cohesive and have a consistent style.

SUMMARY AND CONCLUSION

BUSINESS WRITING

It takes four things to be a good business writer: talent, time, tenacity, and *contacts*. A business writer who knows your industry, knows your medium, has a proven track record, and has functioned full time in the industry for five or six years can usually be trusted to deliver your message on time, on target, and on budget.

BOOK WRITING

It takes four things to make it as an author: talent, time, tenacity, *and luck.* If you're short one or more of these, but feel that the world is waiting to hear some of your thoughts on an important subject, a tale that's running rampant in your mind, or the story of your life, then you're going to have to live with the frustration or find a real writer to help you. (Real writers are those people whose names appear as "with" on the dust jacket. As in, "by Chuck Yeagar *with* Leo Janos," or "by Norman Schwarzkopf *with* Peter Petre.")

If you are famous, you may be able to find a writer to be the "with" for just a percentage of the royalties, without having to pay anything up front. If you're really, really, really famous, the publisher who contacted you can probably find you a writer to be the "with" and pay the up-front costs themselves.

Still, if you have an idea that won't keep, or a need that won't wait for you to develop writing talents of your own, follow the tips and tactics, and you've got a good chance of finding the right person to help you. If a book with your name on it is your goal, you'll have a chance of getting your story published—not as good a chance as you'd have with the lottery, but a chance, nevertheless.

Do You Need an Expert
We Didn't Cover?

If so, we would be happy to include them in a second
volume and will even send you a card when the next
book becomes available. Send your suggestions along
with your name and address to:

Marc Bockmon

Marc Bockmon, Inc.

P.O. Box 3000-240

Georgetown, Texas 78628